Successful
Food
Merchandising
and Display

Successful Food Merchandising and Display

Edited by Martin M. Pegler

Retail Reporting Corporation New York

Retail Reporting Corporation
101 Fifth Avenue,
New York, NY 10003

Distributors to the trade in the United States and Canada:
Van Nostrand Reinhold
115 Fifth Avenue
New York, NY 10003

Distributed outside of the United States and Canada:
Hearst Books International
105 Madison Avenue
New York, NY 10016

Library of Congress Cataloging in Publication Data:
Main Entry under the title: Successful Food Merchandising and Display

Printed and Bound in Hong Kong
Produced by Mandarin Offset
ISBN 0-934590-24-9

Designed by Michael Shroyer

TABLE OF CONTENTS

INTRODUCTION

FOOD is a sensual thing! More than most things, FOOD calls out to our senses—all our senses-and begs to be touched, stroked and fondled. The aroma of FOOD can "drive you mad"—"make you drool"; we can become "slaves" to food—or even "choco-holics." We eat FOOD with our eyes; we devour it even before it reaches our mouths. FOOD can appeal to our sense of hearing; the snap, crackle and pop of some breakfast cereals,—the crisp, crunch of celery,—the snap of a cracker breaking,—or the luscious chomp as we bite into an apple. We have "orgies" with food—and over food. FOOD can be "sinfully" good—and the "first sin" was brought about by FOOD. FOOD has been called "glorious" as in "Food, Glorious Food"; it has even been deified as being "Divine." It is more than sustenance—"our daily bread." It is baguettes, bagels, braided challahs, big black Russian pumpernickels, light and fluffy German kuchens and Syrian pitas large or small. FOOD is essential but FOOD is also a subject of choice and selection. This book is about that choice and selection of FOOD; the glorious, glamourous, and the gourmet as well as the nutritious and the necessary.

This book is also about the presentation of FOOD; how we create the feast for the eye,—the lure and attraction that gets all the other senses to wake up and work up to that ultimate sense—the sense of taste. We will travel from market to supermarket to hypermarket,—from the precious gifts from the earth lovingly laid out on that earth on a brightly woven shawl—to the marble walled interiors of fabled food halls. Our picture journey will lead us into gourmet shops with exquisitely packaged herbs and spices from all over the world—to the herbs and spices spilling out of straw baskets into a crowded selling street in Singapore or a market stall in Narita in Japan. "Food: Markets and Merchandising" will take us into malls and shopping centers and the exciting, colorful food courts,—and transport us to shops, stalls, and kiosks that have foreign and exotic foods—prepared and ready to eat or reheat. We will be able to sit down in patisseries and tea-rooms to sample the eye-delighting tarts and pastries that are being offered for sale up front,—or order a pizza—"to stay" or "to go." We will immerse ourselves in the settings of food; the materials and textures that sell food—promote food, and the lights that make the apples redder—the lettuce seem greener and the cookies "taste" more chocolatey. In this volume, we will analyze the magic of the visual merchandising of food and the design of the enclosure that create the image and set the stage for the appearance of the Glorious Food.

You don't have to imagine the smell of "mom's chocolate brownies" fresh out of the oven,—you can smell that in almost any mall and in some department stores. You can follow your eyes as you turn these pages that revel in and reveal the wonders of food—and then let your imagination supply the aromas; the perfumes and heady, stimulating scents of spices, salamis and aging cheeses. It's a whole world of sights and smells—and we've tried to package it in this volume. So,—"a votre sante"—"eat in good health"—"Salute" —"bon appetite"—"mange, mange" and when it's all done—you won't have gained an ounce but the "eyes will have had it."

MARKETS

"Each night Rome's food came rumbling in on wagons through a fine cobweb of roads; fish caught from the gulfs and the bays, abundant game from the forest, meat and milk from the flocks and herds in the open country. Cheeses, oil, vegetables of every sort; cabbages, lentils, beans and lettuces, radishes and turnips, gourds and pumpkins thundered through the narrow labrinth of streets to the market."

"Consuming Passions," Philippa Pullar

Since earliest times when primitive nomadic tribes met other tribes, in passing, at the wells or watering place in an oasis, there have been markets. There have been places where strangers could meet and peacefully trade or barter the things they had an excess of for the things they needed—be it food or crafts. During the middle ages the market continued to be the central meeting place for people and usually the market was located in a large, open square—often in the center of the town and in the shadow of the main church or cathedral. Sometimes the market was held on special days—sometimes it was a daily occurence, but whichever,—the produce and the food was always fresh and appealingly presented. From the time of the early nomads—through the early civilizations—and the middle ages, the fruits and vegetables,—the cheeses and spices—the freshly baked breads and cakes were presented—on brightly colored shawls or rugs—on scraped and sanded planks of sweet smelling wood—or ornamented hides. Even back then, the food was "prepared"; the fruits were polished, gleaming, soft spots hidden—trimmed with leaves, flowers and arranged in eye-pleasing, colorful mounds.

During the 18th and 19th century some of the larger markets moved indoors and bins and stalls became more formalized and the merchandise was elevated off the ground on to stands or platforms. Now, more than before, people met in the market to shop—to buy or barter—and to discuss politics—talk "of cabbages and kings." Faneuil Hall in Boston dates back to the late 18th century and still functions today as a market—and meeting place. The 19th century witnessed the development of iron and glass enclosures—"Crystal Palaces" of fruits and vegetables—and these were often located near train terminals or landing docks to facilitate the movement of the fragile, perishable merchandise. The Reading Terminal Market dates back almost one hundred years and the Ostermalmshallen in Stockholm is now a venerable centenarium and these two "old timers" are still viable, vital everyday markets and meeting places. Les Halles of Paris is no more and Covent Garden in London functions more as a crafts center than a food market but at least one can see what that glass ceilinged hall must have looked like. Open markets are still with us today—there has been a renaissance of the Outdoor Farmers Market and in many countries around the world, Market Day still means excitement and great expectations.

Today, Market has taken on new meanings. Often under one roof a single owner or corporation will create a Marketplace that not only features fresh produce but, as in day of yore, will feature some prepared foods to tempt and tantalize the shopper—to stimulate the sense with powerful aromas; freshly baked breads or cookies—pots of warming soups—food sizzling and sputtering on charcoal grills—endless salad bars—roasting coffees and more. In this chapter we visit some of the famous old markets and look at some up-dated, upscaled variations on an ancient theme.

Old Kyoto Market, Kyoto, Japan

Typical of many markets is this century old, enclosed marketplace in Kyoto. In a narrow space, actually a road between two rows of houses, this thriving market exists under an iron and glass canopy. Here, as in many European markets that date back for centuries, the produce display is a delight, and each stall is brightly lit, festooned with signs and garlands, personalized by the vendor, and the products are presented with care and affection. The market is a melange of spices and seasonings—as well as the small, everyday "necessities". Whether under a girded skylight of glass and iron or protected by flapping sheets or brightly colored canvas tents or umbrellas,—the market remains the main source for food shopping for millions over the world.

Reading Terminal Market, Philadelphia, PA

Above:
The Farmer's markets are as old as Philadelphia itself. In 1693, the merchants sold their wares down by the Delaware River then they moved up to High Street—now Market Street. It was here that the Reading Terminal Market opened its doors in 1893 and was hailed as one of the great markets of the world along with those in Paris (now gone) and in Stockholm (on the right).

The Market was built by the Railway with a lofty train shed covering two acres of floor space and located to facilitate receiving produce from the outlying farms and for sending fresh foods to customers in the suburbs. It was the first market to have an advanced underground refrigeration system.

Today the market is a blend of merchants and farmers—"a veritable United Nations of ethnic and specialty food vendors and craftsmen." Many of the market's merchants are third or fourth generation tenants and the pride of family tradition enhances the shopping/ eating experience.

In 1888 King Oscar II inaugurated this indoor market. It was designed with high ceilings and enriched with architectural details that were popular at that time and favored by the architect, Gustav Clason. For hundreds of years on the square where the market how stands, outdoor markets thrived. In 1914 a law forbade the sale of meats, cheeses and bread outdoors—and they along with the fruits and vegetables moved inside.

Today over 110 booths are used by more than twenty companies—filling the selling floor with fish, produce, game, baked goods, cheese and coffee. There are also several eating places providing freshly made, tempting dishes. The Market celebrates its 100th birthday and is stronger and more popular than ever.

Ostermalmshallen, Stockholm, Sweden

Quincy Market at Faneuil Hall Marketplace, Boston, MA, developed by The Rouse Co.

Quincy Market has served as a market for the citizens of Boston for over 200 years. The neo-classic structure with colonaded and pedimented facades and domed interior was given new life and meaning by the Rouse Co. twelve years ago when it became the centerpiece of the Faneuil Hall Marketplace development. The Marketplace became the first of what are now called "Festival Centers" which combine the pleasures of eating and food shopping with shopping for clothes—gifts—or just strolling and sight-seeing.

The Quincy Market is a long, narrow building with 75,000 sq. ft. of gross leasable space. The building's space is enhanced by the stalls and cafes outside the building but hugging close to it under yellow, flapping shades. Under the handsome coffered dome that crowns the central rotunda, chairs and tables are provided for the hungry— and the weary. Flanking this area are two long arcaded halls with stalls on either side. The shopper can not only buy produce or freshly baked bread and cookies but dine on a vast assortment of ethnic specialties—or native seafood dishes. Freshly brewed coffees of infinite varieties are always available.

The visitor to Le Faubourg is immediately taken by the openness of this festival marketplace. The whole complex is laid out to be viewed at once—every level from the basement to the 300' atrium. All partition heights between "stores" are restricted to 4'6"—and all baking and food preparation is done out in the open making this a veritable Theatre of Gastronomy.

The shopper smells the bagels still steaming from an open wood oven,—watches luscious gateaux being iced,—exchanges stares with beady eyed fish, or wanders through rows of brightly labeled vintage wines—or vinegars and seasonings.

The exterior architecture of red brick enriched with arches and bright colored banners blends with the feeling of the architecture on old Ste. Catherine St. West. There are three entrances into the light, airy interior and here the architects devised a traffic flow that gives every merchant access to a staircase or an elevator. The most visually pleasing and sensory stimulating shops are up near the entrances. The fruit stalls are in the west end of the building and the boulangerie is at the eastern end. In between, the mall level is filled with butchers, fish-mongers, the delicatessen stands, the cheese-vendors. The uppermost level has myriad fast-food operations along with seating. Floating between the levels—a dining mezzanine where one can sit and see and smell the excitement of the market.

Le Faubourg Ste. Catherine,
Montreal, Que., Canada
Design: Camdi International,
Montreal

Marketplace, Century City Mall, Los Angeles, CA
Developed by: The RREEF Funds

Above:
A new and long awaited addition to the Century City
Shopping Mall in Los Angeles is the Marketplace. It
combines a high ceilinged, airy wood enclosure that
contains freshly prepared foods, produce and fast
foods—with an expanse of verandahs where shoppers may
sit and sip or sup. Fast food operations and restaurants
line up under the assorted colored canvas awning to show
and sell their wares.

The Marketplace addition is rich with "California"
textures and materials; natural woods generously used, red
tiled walks accented with bricks, stucco and everywhere an
abundance of plants and foliage. Glass partitions allow
light through and wooden jalousies add to the "Spanish-
look" and also filter out some of the heat.

Belvedere Square Market, Baltimore, MD
Architect: D.I. Architects, Baltimore

Belvedere Square is a simple steel frame construction with a metal deck and concrete floor slabs built in a Baltimore "neighborhood" that is in the process of gentrification. An abandoned 38,000 sq. ft. department store provided the nucleus for the Market and the architects matched their new constructions to the brick and masonry of the original structure. Within and without there is design harmony. The green canvas awnings unify the facades of the assorted food stalls and shops and within the natural red tile floor blends with the wood valance. Taking the green note from without, the ceiling pipe units, the HVAC elements and the familiar metal shaded lamps are also finished in green.

Stew Leonard, Westport Ave., Norwalk, CT

At the entrance to the sprawling 106,000 sq. ft. market which is set down on 8½ acres of space, a three ton "Rock of Commitment" displays the store's credo. Rule I is: "The customer is always right" and the final summation is "Our business is to create happy customers." This, "the world's largest dairy store" is an Adventureland for Food,—a space walk through miles of fresh produce, foodstuffs and dairy products that come out to greet you on the not quite yellow brick road that wends its way through the many departments. It is never a dull trip. Eight foot tall dogs strum banjos and the Farm Fresh Five sing you along your way to say nought of the morsels you are invited to sample on the way to "Oz." In this no-nonsense, no-glitz, no shine but well lit structure that "jest growed and growed," they report $2,700 in sales for each of their 37,000 sq. ft. of selling space.

The *N.Y. Times* and *Fortune Magazine* call Stew Leonard's "A Disneyland Dairy Store." In addition to the state-of-the-art, audio-and-matronic robots who perform original songs about milk and shopping,—over 55,000 performances a year,—there are cows that moo at the press of a button—and real cows, goats, chickens, sheep and geese to amuse the kids at the Little Farm out front. To add to the fun experience employees, dressed as animals, stroll the aisles.

A market for the new generation of health conscious, diet conscious, ecology conscious and concerned shoppers. Here it is—"The Food—the Whole Food—and Nothing but the Food"—that counts and the management is proud to present a market filled with "just about everything you expect in a major supermarket—all made with wholesome ingredients without chemical additives."

In its New England location,—surrounded by centuries of history and tradition, the shops are bright, light, fresh and attractive, still warm and friendly and at home with the history around them. Daylight pours in over the center of the store where the fresh fruits and vegetables are artfully arrayed under the skylights. In the warmly lit recesses along one perimeter wall—and in the rear, are specialized shops; fish, salads, cheese, meat, and the oven fresh baked goods. A cooking center is near the rear of the store and it is here that food demonstrations are held. The signage is above eye level and facilitates movement inside the store.

Within the retail mall within the up-scaled residential complex is this up-scaled market for time-pressed, urban dwellers. The emphasis is on "boutiques" of specialty foods—and convenience in this one store of 13,000 sq. ft. The "boutiques" are lined up along easy to see and easy to scan arcades and named Floral, Produce, Ethnic Foods, Bakery, Deli, Seafoods, and Liquor while there is still access to general groceries and non-perishable goods.

Presidential Market combines the formality of "Presidential" with the casualness of "Market" and the designers tried to encompass that duality in the store. There is a formal arrangement of alcoves for boutiques— lowered ceilings and intimate lighting as well as individualized fixtures and graphics. In the general area there is a more open feeling with an exposed ceiling, a vaulted space frame, colored banners and HID lighting.

Three of the boutiques are presented with glass storefronts flanked by formal fluted columns and fifty feet of produce can create a colorful background. Moving signs, festive banners and wonderful smells contribute to the exciting shopping experience. Taupe ceramic tile is used throughout and the white ceramic walls are accented with teal.

Jerry Bockwinkel says it is not unique to have groceries in the center of the floor with perishables around the periphery. What is unique is "the level of expense we've gone to portray them." Working with the designers he has created a successful selling environment.

Presidential Market, Presidential Towers,
Chicago, IL
Design: Schafer Assoc., Oak Brook, IL
Photos: Jim Norris

SUPERMARKETS

Supermarkets are a twentieth century phenomenon. They appeared as we know them, shortly after World War I in response to the fast spreading population—the availability of autos to provide mobility to the masses, and the desire, and often need, to get the most for one's money. With the development and growth of Supermarkets where more merchandise—more selections were made available at more and more competitive prices, the unique flavor and charm of the small corner grocery store,—the individually owned and operated mom-and-pop shop began to recede. What disappeared with the small stores—with the grocers who smilingly recognized each customer—knew her special tastes and shopping habits,—who kept a running tally that got paid off weekly or monthly—was Service.

What is surprising is that one of the first "monster operations"—the first Supermarket—began before the Civil War with tea being sold door to door by a salesman/proprietor with a horse drawn cart. In 1861 that business became a specialty tea-selling shop in a tiny space along the wharves of N.Y. harbor where the Twin Towers now stand in Lower Manhattan. It was a partnership between the horse and wagon salesman, George Huntington Hartford and the "incredible showman," George F. Gilman,—a man of foresight who named the infant business "The Great American Tea Company." The basic sales principle was simple; make tea more accessible to the masses by direct buying, on the part of the retailer,—eliminating the middleman and making only a small profit per pound, but selling many store pounds. Hartford's conviction that the way to grow was to treat customers fairly and earn their trust and confidence went along with Gilman's vision and flair to promote the business. With the opening of the West, and to commemorate the event, the small tea company became "The Great Atlantic & Pacific Tea Co." By 1878 there were over 100 retail outlets extending out to Chicago and beyond, and by 1880 the product line was expanded to include coffee, sugar, spices, canned milk, butter plus a private label line of food stuffs that included A&P baking powder and 8 O'clock

coffee. Before World War I, there were over 4000 stores in existence carrying an extensive product line, but by now the unnecessary selling expenses were eliminated including credit selling, home deliveries, telephone orders, stamps, premiums—and even advertising. The chain, in 1927, had grown to 15,000 stores "Where Economy Rules"—and standardization was the key ingredient to rapid expansion.

Today's Supermarkets are succeeding because, in so many instances, they are turning back the clock and returning to Service—to individual attention—responding to customers' wants as well as needs. A&P is still one of the leaders in the field and their new Future Store represents what the customer has to expect in food shopping experiences—and environments. In many successful operations besides the traditional grocery, meat, dairy and general merchandise—one finds "boutiques"—special food areas; bakeries on the premises,—freshly caught fish,—gourmet cheese shops with many exotic selections,—extensive delicatessens and prepared foods to go,—Sushi Bars,—Taco Stands—fast foods—salad bars and cafes. "Bulk Food" has become, for some, a way of shopping and supermarkets have tastefully created Bulk Food Galleries. Signage plays an important part in the store design and the graphics and decor—the color and light all add to that shopping experience.

Where do we go from here? Some Retail soothsayers speak of the Hypermarket as the Supermarket of the future; more than a grocery—more like a discount department store with an in depth stock of foods, clothes plus services. Whatever comes through however—one thing is certain—the shopper will be served. Today's shoppers include the singles shopping for one,—the working woman and/or her mate—or the teenager shopping for the family—and all, in common, lack time and desire convenience and selection. Future Supermarket strategies will be directed toward answering the key demographic questions—and providing more exciting—more interesting more attractive selling spaces.

The Super Center spreads out over 60,000 sq.ft and features many specialty areas including Le Gourmet (prepared gourmet food), A cheese and a floral shop, meat and fish areas, as well as a full service bank, a video-tape rental department, a pharmacy and a one hour film processing service. There is also a fast food cafe.

The color scheme is white, red and charcoal gray with gleaming accents of chrome. The personnel wear red and gray aprons and the shoppers get gray carts to fill. The interior is spacious and well lit; neon signage, frosted glass incandescent lamps for accents and fluorescents for back-up.

The venerable old supermarket chain has become the NEW supermarket as it presents its new graphic bright face to the public. Drawing on the experiences learned in other 40,000 sq. ft. shops, the company and the designers have been able to create this new look with an improved layout, store design and lighting techniques—and a greater customer appeal.

The interior is sparkling light and bright—all black and white with handsome contrasting graphics calling out across long aisles to announce what is to be found along the perimeter walls. The lighting combines HID with incandescents for a pleasant overall effect that also enhances the color of the produce. The gondola lighting was "computerized" by the designers to provide even light levels to all shelves—top and bottom. At the cash/wrap area a lower ceiling and softer lighting supplies a sense of intimacy to customers and employees.

Not only is A&P upgrading their image on the selling floor, but also in the private label product assortment in terms of content and packaging—"to elevate our quality standards and customer perception." Indeed, it is a "Proud New Feeling."

A&P, Futurestore, Rockville Centre, NY
Design: Robert P. Gersin and Assoc., NY

A&P Food Bazaar, Union Square, NY

Left: The 30,000 sq. ft. gourmet-oriented supermarket opened at 14th St. and Park Ave. So. in the historic Union Square district which is now in the sweep of ''gentrification.'' It was designed by the A&P company to meet the varied needs of consumers in the surrounding neighborhood by providing a complete supermarket offering enhanced by top flight service and a wide array of gourmet and specialty foods. The Food Bazaar's range of products are framed by an elegant decor utilizing muted pastels and service departments arranged and decorated as individual boutiques. The lighting is low and pleasant.

A&P Food Emporium, Upper Broadway, NY

Above: In rehabbing a former supermarket into a Food Emporium, The A&P company turned the 21,000 sq. ft. operation into a sparkling showcase for traditional groceries joined with gourmet foods. It is located in the lower level of a block long condominium only blocks from Lincoln Center. Inside, the shopper is in an "open market" with a handsome presentation of fresh fruits and vegetables and all the expected—plus some "unexpecteds" like a demo kitchen where celebrity "how to" cooking shows are staged. The walls and floor are warm white and flushed with the warm light on the assembled products. The pink terrazzo floors blend with the terra cotta tiled aisles.

This highly competitive chain of full line supermarkets planned to expand its market share through new
stores and a vast remodeling program. This is the
prototype for the new look; a new package design which
includes a comprehensive graphics program and a
"cohesive corporate identity through a cohesive looking
environment."

Soft appetizing colors were used for a warm and friendly
atmosphere. The graphic cues, a checkerboard system of
cornices mirrored by a checkerboard floor patterned
border, encourage the customer to cover the whole selling
floor. Department names blend neon script with solid
lettering. The promotional and informational sign system
is consistent throughout, and endless signposts that
combine food categories with photographs and banners
with words and pictures.

Lucky Stores, San Francisco, CA
Design: Walker Group/CNI, NY
Photos: Toshi Yoshimi

This prototype was designed for a supermarket/hypermarket that sells everything from fine jewelry to family apparel to food. The design called for an appeal to the Californian customer base; a tasteful and enjoyable—yet efficient shopping experience in a store that is price and value driven.

The store feels free and spacious with broad aisles, high ceilings and wide shallow departments. A pastel color scheme with bright accents contribute to the store's personality. Interior signage is bright and colorful and furthers the strong graphic image. The decorative color treatments, graphic and lighting solutions made the store affordable within a limited budget.

Gemco, Rowland Heights, CA
Design: Walker Group/CNI, NY
Photos: Toshi Yoshimi

Ito-Yokado, Co., Ltd., Tsudanuma, Narashino-Shi,
Chiba, Japan

This, the largest supermarket in Japan is located in a suburb of Tokyo. The food department covers almost 31,000 sq. ft. and is part of a hypermarket of sorts that also carries clothing and household supplies. The store is an interesting blend of contemporary, ultra-today methods and materials along with traditional Japanese customs and selling rituals. The lighting, throughout, in true Japanese shopping style is light and bright fluorescents with incandescent spots added where the product or produce needs the extra "warmth." In addition to the meat, dairy and packaged products there is an abundance of pre-packaged, ready-to-go meals and spices and seasonings available in bulk.

Traditionally dressed employees stand behind some counters to prepare and serve the food—customized to the shoppers request. In the freshly baked foods area, the saleswomen wear simple white smocks with matching haircoverings. The Bakery is a contemporary, glass enclosed shop and in the fruit and vegetable section the shopper can have her selected produce blended into a refreshing drink to enjoy there—or to take home.

A supermarket with a flair that is not only called Fiesta, but is an ongoing Ethnic Fiesta. Located in west Houston, it reaches out to a wide range of customers; Latin American from Mexico and as far away as Chile and Argentina,—and Oriental/Asians from Japan, China and Vietnam. In its International scope, the store invites its shoppers to not only buy products and produce that are part of their ethnicity, but to sit or stand and try some variations on their food—or the foods of their neighbors.

The store, in white ceramic tile, accented with red tiles and the happy red color—dear to both the Latinos and the Orientals—appears throughout on fixtures, signs, chair seats and table tops. Even the space struts that swing across the ceiling are painted red. Over the perimeter counters, shops and fast-food operations the ceilings are dropped and the lighting is warmer and more intimate than the HIDs that illuminate the center of the store.

The Sushi Bar is new at Fiesta Mart and is located near the fresh fish section. The snack bar that features the Fajitas (marinated and grilled strips of meat wrapped in tortillas) is popular and the aroma from the wood fire where the fajitas are prepared brings shoppers from all through the store.

Fiesta Mart, W. Houston, TX

Tianguis (teeONgeese) is the Aztec word for marketplace and the vast Von empire of food stores has created this particular concept for the rapidly growing Hispanic community of Southern California. The selection of foods is targeted towards Spanish/Mexican cuisine but there is also a full range of traditional dry groceries, fresh produce, seafoods and staples.

Signage is in Spanish and English and the employees are bilingual. The snack bar is built in what might be a Mexican shopping square and the specialty food departments include a Torilleria, a Carnicerie, a Panaderia, and a Salchichoneria. The lighting is warm and on target and red, orange, yellow and green/blue colors are used to liven up the store interior.

Von's Tianguis, Montebello, L.A., CA

Von's Pavilion, Garden Grove, CA

Above: *Forbes Magazine* described Pavilion as "a mix of playground, packaging and theater in a high volume food store." The store is about 50,000 sq. ft. of selling space and offers produce, meat and seafood, prepared foods, a hot bakery, gourmet coffee shop and more. The layout emphasizes food related products of department store quality and is targeted at customers who are concerned with quality and nutrition, have limited time and prefer the convenience of one stop shopping.

The on-site preparation of foods, the innovative signing and the well planned layout create an air of excitement for up-scaled shoppers.

Von's Pavilion, Garden Grove, CA

39

Provigo Store, Montreal, Que. Canada
Design: Camdi International, Montreal

Up in Canada, in the midst of a general "upscaling"—the 30 year old chain of Provigo Conventional stores are scheduled for an "upgrading". In this prototype store, the market is being brought "more into line with today's lifestyles—with all of these boutique approaches. The stores are service oriented and warm."

The store's interior colors are gentle and muted and the all important signage is in a refined Belle Epoque style. Latticework and colored canvas canopies over the service departments and the open metal grids over the produce and bulk foods contribute to the open, airy and spacious feel of the store. Spotlights, attached to the overhead elements, bring a warm glowing light onto the produce for sale.

The many boutiques include fresh fish, a bakery, a boucherie and a charcuterie. The produce and bulk foods are presented in an old world ambience that is friendly and even the signs invite the shopper to "Veuillez"—to try—the goods.

41

Von's Grocery, Las Vegas, NE
Design: Design Forum, Dayton, Ohio

The Von's Grocery company has grown from a small market in downtown Los Angeles—started in 1906— to probably the largest supermarket chain in Southern California; an area that spans from Fresno to the Mexican border and from Las Vegas to the Pacific Ocean.

Each of the four major divisons of Von's appeals to and approaches a different segment of the shopping public. On the previous pages we presented two of their more specialized divisions and here is the Grocery which is a supermarket that combines a food store with a drug store operation.

A smart script signage identifies the various departments and divisions on the selling floor. The fluorescent luminaires in the ceiling provide the general light, but the hundreds of spots that line the facades of the perimeter shops or are attached to the suspended metal frames over the produce in the center of the floor bring the merchandise into full, glowing color. The color scheme is sophisticated and fresh, and the general ambience is welcoming.

Shoprite, Yonkers, NY
Design: Planned Expansion Grp.
Architects/Planners, P.C., White Plains, NY

This prize winning store of 45,000 sq. ft. is truly an outstanding achievement in supermarket design. It was one of the first to bring sense and sensitivity to the lighting requirements of the market selling floor—putting the right color on the product—bringing the merchandise to the shopper's attention—and doing it economically and attractively.

Using its background in specialty store design, the architects/designers devised a lighting plan that would work along with a color, graphics and signage strategy. The store is color coded; green for produce, red for meat, yellow for dairy and blue for fish. These brightly colored perimeter walls provide a bright environment and also make it easy to find what one wants—from a distance. The perimeter walls were lowered to 10' for a more intimate and personal scale and that also brought the light down closer to the products presented. Linear light tubes were hung 8' above the display tables and counters that stood away from the wall units—and restated the color of the area. Fluorescents were set behind colored baffles that were lowered over the perimeter areas.

The center area where the groceries were stacked was left neutral under a 14' ceiling and the color of the packages were allowed to take over. Here, direct product illumination was provided by fluorescent lamps set into a fascia strip about 8'' out from the gondola.

Some shimmer—lots of shine—and the sparkle of colored neon signs add up to the look of the Giant supermarket. Giant was an early pioneer in the supermarket "game" when it made its first appearance in 1936 in the Washington, D.C. area. Its concept of high volume based on offering customers a wide variety of quality food at the lowest possible prices—and friendly pleasant service has been the reason for its success and expansion through Virginia, Maryland and the District area.

Lower ceilings, better lighting, food beautifully presented, a fabulous fresh salad bar plus an extraordinary Bulk food boutique of bushel baskets under a metal arcade lined with yellow spots are only some of the "draws" for shoppers and the area. The white floors reflect the light—the polished ceilings cast back reflections, and the multi neon signs call out to the customers on the 50,000 sq. ft. floor.

In addition to the bright, cheerful and friendly feeling of the store, Giant is also noted for its half-price specials and super-specials—always highlighted, and its drug departments. There is nothing cut-rate in the store design and visual presentation.

Giant, Maryland & Virginia

Krogers Store of the 90's, Cincinnati, OH
Design: Retail Planning Assoc., Columbus, OH
Architect: Hixson, Inc., Cincinnati, OH

This easy-to-shop, life-style environment uses its ambience to target the particular shopper segments. Destination departments are clearly defined to draw the shopper into and through the 62,000 sq. ft. store, and the designers used neon scripting in a muted, contemporary color-coordinated palette—as well as boutique style departmentalization to make things work.

In the right front corner of the store is a 48 seat cafe followed by the Deli. On the opposite side of the entrance is the Service Bakery followed by the Floral stall. The back wall features seafood and dairy. Also, towards the front of the store there is a pharmacy, an HBA department, a dry cleaner, video film rental service, and even a financial center.

The "boutiquing" of the space helps achieve a more human scale for the selling floor. A checkerboard theme is incorporated into the Deli, the Cafe and Fresh Catch seafood areas. Coral tile accents and teal blue (in seafood) contemporize the color palette. Taupe, soft light gray walls, gray and white floors and the warm gray ceiling serve as background for the accent colors. Lensed fluorescents and incandescent spots are set into the pattern textured ceiling.

Hypermarket, Garland, TX
Design: Retail Planning Associates, Columbus, OH

Two price-dominated retail formats,—food and general merchandise, are incorporated into a giant space of 220,000 gross sq. ft. to become a "mall without walls" and feature Wal-Mart's "narrow but deep off-price assortment of first quality brand name merchandise."

The interior layout includes power display aisles, large graphic banners, towers with price-value messages, a color coordinated point of sale system, directional kiosks and, in the food area, neon signs. The store is organized into color coded merchandise worlds, and the floor tile colors are used to distinguish one "world" from another. The high, barrel-vaulted, ceilings, the arches, the exterior and front mallways are reminiscent of Grand Central Station. Glazed concrete blocks and colored metal roofing were used for economy.

The bold graphics along with the neon signs distinguish the green coded food area. Included in this area is a bakery capable of turning out one thousand loaves of bread an hour, a tortilla factory, a fresh and frozen seafood shop and a deli.

A 31,000 sq. ft. food court with a seating capacity of two hundred houses nineteen non-competing food concessions. This is big—really big!

SPECIALTY STORES

"Serenely full, the epicure would say, 'Fate cannot harm me,—I have dined today.'"
Sydney Smith, 1771-1845

An epicure is a person who takes pleasure in and enjoys well prepared food and drink,—and it would seem we are becoming a nation of epicures,—of gourmets—of connoisseurs. Our palates can distinguish between "hamburger A and Hamburger B,"—our noses sniff out the coffee bean flavored with a touch of Amaretto—a soupcon of mocha—a hint of cinnamon. This is the Time of the Maven—the expert, the specialist. The "maven" knows which chocolate chip cookie is the most chocolatey and chippiest; which candy is the richest, creamiest and freshest. With the educated nose to lead the way and the eye taking in the variety of offerings spread out under flattering lights in an ambience that enhances the product, the maven seeks out choices —looks for adventures in sampling—variations on the theme—for selection. Specialty stores have become boutiques that specialize in particular foodstuffs and carry an in-depth selection of that food—plus the go-withs to delight the consumer.

Way, way back, only the rich could afford specialty foods and the masses had to do with bread—if they could find it. There is nothing plebian about bread for this Yuppie generation; this consumer wants a choice. She/He wants a choice of grains—a variety of shape and sizes to choose from and exotic origins to enhance the bread-tasting experience. Today's consumer does not live by the bread alone—but also by the how, why, what and where of the bread—and especially the when it was baked. The contemporary shopper in the mall—in the commuter railroad station—in the neighborhood strip center is more affluent, more educated, more traveled, and more "pampered and spoiled" by food retailers than ever before. Food is part of many lifestyles and an expression of who and what that shop-

per is,—and where she/he is going. The specialty stores that sell to these customers must also reflect the same up-scale attitude—the smartness and sophistication in their decor and presentation.

In this chapter we will visit a few of the Boutiques. We have selected some candy shops that appear in malls—in rehabbed warehouses and on main streets. Breads are baked in bakeries—and the bakeries are quite varied from home and hearth operations to slick and sharp Continental designs. The "Cookie Monster" that lurks in malls has a choice too, and the entries in this chapter show a variety of selling approaches in their presentation and their store design. Bulk Food shopping is something rather new and, so far, the popular items sold in bulk—in free standing operations and also in Supermarkets are candies, spices and myriad variations on "trail mixes." Coffee and Tea specialty shops range from kiosks to stands to full scale emporiums. Another new taste-tempter in an up-swing for the upscale shopper is the Pasta Shop where the harried and the hurrying can select from hundreds of shapes, sizes, semolinas and seasonings. In some situations, the shopper must seek out the traditional, family-flavored shop—rich in smells, sights and nostalgia while other shops are light, bright and as sassy fresh as the Pasta that comes out to meet the scurrying commuter.

This chapter should leave no doubt that within the same specialties there are choices—there are differences —and the shopper does have a selection. No longer does she say "Cheese," now she savors, smacks and smiles to say "Camembert," "Brie,", "Stilton"—and even "low fat, low sodium, low cholesterol, please."

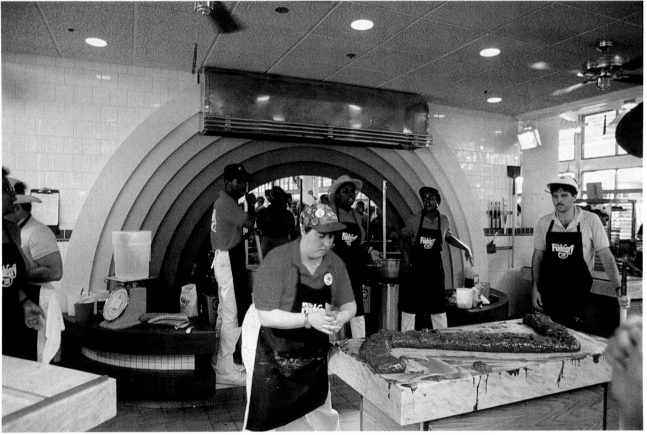

The Fudgery, Bayside, Miami, FL
The Rouse Co.

Kron Chocolatier, Great Neck, NY   Design: Mojo/Stumer, Architects, Great Neck, NY
Photo: Phillip Ennis, Baldwin, NY

Above: In a minute space with a limited budget, the designers created a warm and welcoming ambience using variations on the chain's familiar color scheme. The narrow shop was planned to accommodate the making, the selling and the stocking of the chocolates. The candy making and chocolate dipping equipment was set up front to serve as a come-on and as an up-front display attraction to the shoppers on the street. The pinks, mauves and lavenders flatter the product, and the long mirrored wall on one side seems to "open" up the space. The shelved walls, on the opposite side, are adaptable and have high visual accessibility.

Right: As traditional as the product is the store design for the Hershey shop. The floor is paved in small white tiles banded in a rich chocolate brown with the firm name inlaid,—reminiscent of the soda fountains and candy shoppes of the turn-of-the-century. The fixtures are of oak, enriched with chamfered panels and a hearty crown molding outlines the perimeter of the shop and the zig-zag the counter makes in the small space. A provincial patterned paper, also in chocolate brown, covers the walls. The incandescent downlights suffuse the area in warmth. Note the "old-fashioned" touches; the candy jars to the right of the entrance and the nostalgic two wheeled cart behind.

54

Hershey's, National Place, Washington, DC
Design: Babcock-Schmidt, Bath, OH
Photo: Jim Maguire, Akron, OH

Purdy's Chocolates, Bellevue Square, Bellevue, WA
Design: Callison Partnership, Seattle, WA
Photos: Robert Pisano

Far Left: For its open mall location, the Canadian based chocolatier requested increased circulation and "more presence" in the mall. New casework and circulation patterns were designed, creating an easily accessible, highly visible "storefront." The two brushed brass towers enclose glass shelves, featuring the packaged product, and also appear to support the gray "roof" that brings the shop down to human-size scale. The cases are covered with a pale, pale mauve-pink laminate trimmed with natural oak and the brushed brass of the tower is repeated as detailing and banding on the counters. The light natural oak also serves for counter tops and panel appliques on the central display case. All lighting is incandescent with some MR16 accent lights,—all contained under the "eaves" of the roof. Over the towers,—more light—directed down on the displayed merchandise.

Above: This retail outlet was designed for a bulk wholesaler of chocolate products and it is located in the downtown manufacturing facility. The designers opted to utilize many of the old "factory" textures like the wood floors, the lofty beamed ceiling and the brick walls,—to reinforce the image of the firm's long standing tradition of quality. The theme was enhanced by using a conveyor and industrial drums as display props. This was to remind the shopper of the freshness—the just-made quality of the candy. High-Tech grids continue the factory look as they are used on the walls and as open-faced stacking display cubes. Lighting throughout was a serious problem; how to light the space without melting the chocolates. A successful plan was arrived at.

Munson's Chocolates, Trumbull Shopping Park,
Trumbull, CT

The Chocolate Dipper, Marketplace Center, Boston, MA
Design: Stephen Faulk and Assoc., Boston, MA

Left: An open-to-the-mall shop enriched with a marble facade and matching marble tiled floors. The shop is color schemed in medium gray teamed up with coral and dubonnet for a fine, rich statement—and a complement to the chocolate. In addition to the fluorescent luminaires over the selling space, the ceiling is dotted with incandescent floods and spots on mini tracks to supply the "pow" lighting on the product display. In the center, a display platform that is changed with the many promotional thrusts. The wall opposite the selling counter is composed of gray laminate wall fixtures with glass shelves against a glowing peach/pink wall.

Above: A chic, super elegant chocolate shop; warm white, rich glowing polished woods and a generous dash of black and white marble. The 850 sq. ft. space is long and narrow and the design is split up into three bays lengthwise. Up front, a marble slab near the projecting bay window, where the chocolates are made. The marketing part of the shop combines the marble with granite floors in a series of rectangles and a vaulted ceiling stretches above, the sweep echoed by the swelling curve on the mahogany and glass case on the right. The architects describe the central bay as a "shrine—the almost religious attraction people have towards chocolate." The bay windowed facade consists of mahogany accented with stainless steel and etched glass; a contemporary but classic feeling.

Baker Meister, New Park Mall, Newark, CA
Design: Babcock-Schmidt, Bath, OH
Photos: Jim Maguire, Akron, OH

J.P.'s French Bakery, New York, NY
Design: Charles Morris Mount, Inc., NYC

Left: A touch of the Victorian—and the flavor of grandma's home baked cookies: a wooden facade of squared pilasters and multi-mullioned windows, and within a fascia of fan windows filled with etched and colored glass. Not quite Steamboat Gothic but the architectural details do step the shop's "look" back to another time. An early 20th century inspired wallpaper wraps the walls. Hand decorated tiles accent the white ceramic tile covered oven that fills most of the rear wall. The front glass counter with sloping front also is "period" inspired. The floor is paved with country style, terra cotta tiles. Nostalgia appeals to all the senses at Baker Meister.

Above: The wood facade with brass trim and the black and gold sign overhead looks "Parisian" and within the ambience is light, bright and bakery fresh. Etched glass light shades hang down from the "old" embossed tin ceiling. Terra cotta tiles cover the floor and the counter and cabinets repeat the woodwork of the facade. The walls are white and unadorned. Additional spots, along the fascia over the shelves, provide the highlights on the baked goods. Here too, a clever and sophisticated use of cliches creates a special environment—"Paris" bakery as the New Yorker thinks it looks.

Wilton Enterprises, Arlington Heights, IL   Design: Design Forum, Dayton, OH

Bagel Emporium, Bayside, Miami, FL   A Rouse Co. Development

Patisserie De La Loire, Les Halles D'Anjou, Montreal, Que., Canada
Design: Optima Design, Montreal, Que., Canada

Far Left: Wilton Bakery is more than a cake shop,—it is an invitation to a wedding, an anniversary, a party,—any celebration. Party cakes are what they sell along with the makings and fixings; invitations, partyware, decorating supplies, etc. Designed in pale gray, mauve and coral—plus white, the festive setting is flattering to party planning patrons. Cake designs are shown in a gallery—enhanced by giant graphics of the products and video selections played on conveniently located monitors. The Wilton specialists offer their products in a setting that is sugar coated and iced post-modernism.

Above: A small space makes a big bagel statement as it sends up aromatic smoke signals from the bake oven visible behind. The "swiss-cheese" counter allows the bagel varieties to be seen but not touched. The overhead giant bagels graphically reach out—with the scent—into the mall.

Left: 500 sq. ft. of visual excitement. The gray stepped design frames the rear service wall—and part of the front counter. Under the shaped fabric awning, a standing display case supported by "columns" capped in gray and rose/mauve. The same column motif guards the ends of the shop. The actual bake oven is behind the service wall but still visible from out front.

Cheryl's Cookies, Parmatown Mall, Cleveland, OH
Design: Richardson Smith, Worthington, OH

The Original Cookie Co., Puente Hills Mall, City of Industry, CA
Design: Original Cookies & Friel Bernheim, Philadelphia, PA

Far Left: "The red and black store design reflects the dynamic personality of the business and the people who run it,"—and the prototype design has garnered awards for the company that designed it. In addition to the freshly-baked-on-the-premises cookies, there are baskets, coffee mugs, gift tins of cookies, homemade ice-cream, and gourmet coffees. In order to have and to hold—and show that many items, the designers created a dual level shop in the mall with the cookies, coffee and ice-cream at the mall level on the black and white checkerboarded floor and the gift items raised up on a wooden floor with white laminate and glass fixtures to hold them. The walls are painted bright red and incandescents make the area glow.

Above: Red, white and green—done in ceramic tiles and tied in with natural oak. The area is bright, light and gleaming white with the decorative bands of red and green breaking up the white with directional patterns that lead to the product display. Overhead incandescents illuminate the stock of cookies in this 500 sq. ft. open shop. The stainless steel oven is prominent on the rear wall.

The Famous Chocolate Chip Cookie, Quaker Bridge, Trenton, NJ
Design: Q-5, Wayne, NJ

SPEARS

CHECK POINT

NUTS & MIXES

PICK & MIX

MEDIUM BAGS

SMALL BAGS

SALTER 40

WEIGHTS INDICATED
ARE APPROXIMATE
ONLY. ACCURATE
WEIGHTS WILL BE
GIVEN AT CHECKOUT

Spears, London, England
Design: Isherwood and Co., London

Bulk, Loehmann Plaza, St. Petersburg, FL

Far Left: With the popularity of "pick and pack your own" products, Bulk shops are appearing as areas in supermarkets (see Giant), in malls and on main street. Spears in London was designed throughout by Isherwood and Co.; from logostyle to signage to store facade, visual displays, graphics and fixturing. The visual impact of the "bulk" products is most important and the mechanics of self-help,—the scoop, the bags, the scale and the ties must be readily available for a smooth operation. This shop is white from floor to ceiling with accents of orange and teal green.

Above: A high-tech design in a small enclosed mall. Green grids are used to create a fascia up-front and to separate the plastic bins into food categories on the floor. The same green is used on the signage that competes for air space with large photo-graphics. A dropped green metal track sports spots that light up the salmon back wall. Simple, efficient and effective.

Left: A more rustic, down-country approach for candies and sweets—in bulk. The sanded wood floor is covered with clean wood barrels and an oak fascia comes down from the ceiling. Dark green fabric wraps around the exposed wall,—a foil for the candy displays. Spots on tracks alternate with fluorescent fixtures to provide a pleasant light in the store.

Candy Barrel, Galleria, Baltimore, MD

Coffeeworks, Willow Brook Mall, NJ
Design: Dorf Associates, NYC

Above: Behind a classic-inspired facade of natural wood highlighted with copper bands and stripes is a shop filled with coffee, coffee scents—and more wood. The interior combines the natural wood floor and wall fixtures with gridded laminate cubes on the floor. A richer hunter green is used as the accent color and a series of arch shaped nylon banners, hanging from the ceiling and stretching across the store, lead to the green sign boards and the all important coffee bar in the rear.

Right: The small, semi-circular counter of pink tinted wood banded in brass is backed up by a fabric covered screen—also pink. In the very limited space a variety of teas are attractively presented.

Far Right: This is one of a growing chain of Gourmet Coffee shops—a shop of about 750 sq. ft. with an old fashioned "general store" look. The facade is painted green and enriched with moldings and architectural details,—and the windows of beveled glass recall another era. Inside, custom oak fixtured banded with brass railings and topped with white stand out from the green painted walls. An oak fascia, dimensionalized with molding frames, bring "down" the ceiling to a more intimate level. The shop is filled with charm and warmth and a tiny bar serves "coffee and."

Jen's Tea, Les Cours Mont Real, Montreal, Que., Canada
Design: Optima Design, Montreal, Que., Canada

Gloria Jean's Coffee Bean
Headquarters in Arlington Hts, IL

Left: A sophisticated shop for the sophisticated wine shopper who is profiled as predominantly male, 25-45, with high disposable income and a highly developed self-image. The exterior is simple; a white stone finish with three large windows with blue and green colored glass above and rough timber "storeraisers" below. Inside,—a traditional but contemporary feeling. Original floor boards were stained a warm russet color to set off the walls plastered with natural terra cotta and lacquered. A specially designed racking system uses traditional materials in a "contemporary and witty way." The uprights are twisted, concrete reinforcing rods set into deep stained birdseye maple. Most of the bottles are stored horizontally except the sample bottle which is angled towards the customers. The arched overhead lighting elements reinforce the "wine cellar" image.

Esprit Du Vin, London, England
Design: Fitch & Co., London, England

70

The Wine Center, Crown Center, Heartland Market, Kansas City, MO
Design: Philip George Associates, NYC

Above: The facade—a colorful post-modern expression in blue and green with an art deco inspired doorway in terra cotta. Inside,—a more traditional approach to selecting wines. The wood wall units are painted the same rich terra cotta color and the hanging, frosted glass lamps add to the warm, intimate feeling. The small mullioned window recalls an 18th century inn or tavern and the arched sweep over the window suggests the arched "cave" ceilings of the fine wine cellars. The stock bottles lie horizontally behind the sample bottles up front.

71

Pasta Via, Denver, CO
Design Concept: John Mullins, pres.

Pasta is popular and getting even more popular with today's health and diet aware consumers. Here we present two fine but different approaches to the presentation of Pasta.

On this page: Pasta Via is commuter-oriented. The shops are often located where people on the move can stop and shop for prepared, ready-to-travel salads and dishes—or for the "fixings" to make a dish from "scratch". There are also tables for those who want immediate gratification in this light, warmly lit, tile-covered interior of about 600 sq.ft.

Right: Trio's is located in the North End of Boston in a friendly family-oriented Italian neighborhood where "old time" values provide the ambience and the decor. Though the products are presented with old world charm in woven baskets, wooden trays and in glass bell jars—the fixtures are high-tech. The hand lettered "signage", the clutter and "mange-mange" spirit goes with the faded family portraits, framed momentos and flags that are interspersed by scrawled chalk-board specials,—and they are all part of Trio's charm.

Trio's, Boston, MA

73

GOURMET SHOPS

"Food was material to carve, mold into shapes, colour, turn to different textures. Cuisine was an art form for which enjoyment the epicure must employ all his senses; the eye to delight in the appearance, the nose to savour the aroma, the palate to experience the textures and juicy succulence, the ear to attend internally to the crispness of pastry, the crunchiness of nuts, the smooth frothiness of souffles."

Ben Johnson (1572-1637) on 17th cent. cooks

There have always been persons who were born with the equivalent of a silver spoon in their mouths—and enough silver in their pockets to keep that silver spoon, fork and knife in constant contact with only the best—the finest—the most unique and exquisite. The kind of food you eat—the food you serve and how that food is prepared and presented—has always been an indication of who and what you are and where you belong or "niche-in" in the many strata of society. According to Peter Farb and George Armelagos in "Consuming Passions"—"The quality of the meal and its setting conveys a more subtle social message than anything that is consciously verbalized." For centuries persons have used food to impress others; the wedding feasts that lasted for days—the fatted calf—the gifts of grain and oil—the epicurean feasts or eating orgies of the Romans—even to the baking of four and twenty vocalizing blackbirds in a pie to set before the king—down to our business lunches where the deal is more often based on the palate—the pate and the pastries—rather than the facts and figures, graphs and charts.

In days of yore—and well before that—the cooks and chefs reveled in the preparation of unusual and unexpected dishes,—concocted with hard-to-get fruits, birds or animals,—flavored with rare and exotic spices and seasonings,—and served up on silver and gilt palavers, chased tureens or stuffed in a feathered peacock. The more creative chefs spent even more time on how the dish would be "presented" than on the actual preparation and cooking of the dish. Therefore, today, equal with the taste of the gourmet food is the preparation—the packaging and presentation of the luxury items.

With the growth of the Nouveau Riche—of the burgeoning middle class into monied, upwardly mobile—spend-and-be-noticed—new society of the 19th century, we find the development of institutions that catered to those who could afford "the best." To sell "the best" it had to be shown in an elegant setting—a rich ambience that exuded the good taste and exclusivity of the products being offered. In 1886, Auguste Fauchon opened up his fine grocery shop on the Place de la Madeleine which became one of the most famous "luxury grocers" in the world. It became the mecca for the gourmet—the epicure—the silver-palated few and the monied many. Under new management since 1967, Fauchon has become a world-wide "collector"—"an authentic gastronomie library containing the best that each country has to offer." Today Fauchon is, above all, French Gastronomy, with an offering of Grand Cuisine able to satisfy the most demanding palate. Fortnum and Mason started as a stall in a doorway in Picadilly, in London, in 1707 but by 1788 had a grip on the luxury trade.

They were selling "boned portions of poultry and game in aspic jelly, decorated with lobsters and prawns, eggs in brandy soaked cake with whipped cream, mince pies, etc.—and all decorated and prepared so as to require no cutting." Today Fortnum and Mason is still THE finest grocer in London and plans to be "rocketing game pies in refrigerated boxes to the edge of the universe, providing hampers for space shuttle travellers, and advising customers on the best tea to suit the waters of the moon."

For those who can't get to London or Paris, we visit some of our own new Gourmet Grocers—who bring the world's finest to you—wherever you are—with elegance—with panache—and with presentation.

Joseph Burke Ltd.,New York, NY
Architect: Al D'Oreo
Interior Design: Ota Rocha

This is the house built for the epicure to delight in. For over 100 years this has been the place to find the most elegant and exotic of foods and spices—collected from all over the world and presented with panache. The showcase —the interior—is all fine rich woods and pink marbles. In addition to the multitude of cooks and pastry chefs that daily prepare the exquisite dishes that delight the eye and please the palate, there are visual merchandisers who set out the daily array of specialty foods and keep the selling floor a show-place.

Throughout the store one senses the "tradition"—the lineage and heritage—the sense of security and "class." The main store carries groceries, wines and spirits, gourmet foods, cheeses, fruits and vegetables in 500 sq. meters. The annex (150 sq. meters) is housed by the confectionary, the bakery and pastry shop and a charming cafe.

Fauchon, Place de la Madelaine, Paris, France

Fortnum & Mason, London, England

Left: Classic and classy is Fortnum & Mason,—a long and steady development from the original stall in a Piccadilly doorway in 1707 to the gourmet shop—"Grocers and Provision Merchants to the Queen." It is an institution where fine foods and fruits are elegantly presented amidst marble, gleaming wood, architectural moldings and details of past centuries and sparkling crystal/gilt chandeliers. The deep red carpet is laid out for the shoppers who are invited to peruse and feast (only with the eyes) the assembled provisions. The ground floor staff continues to carry out their duties in morning coats—and it is "white glove" treatment all the way at Fortnum & Mason.

Above: One of the fine departments in the new 72,000 sq. ft. flagship store is this Fine Foods area. The floors are pink and ceramic tiles inset with patterns and borders of black and pink marble. The floor fixtures are oriental inspired matte black lacquered units and the wall units are separated by red lacquered columns. Signage banners are suspended from the ceiling—a series of levels that carry the incandescent lamps. Fine art and sculpture are incorporated into the gracious design of the shop.

Dean & DeLuca, Prince St., NYC

The surroundings couldn't be simpler; old white tiled floors, white walls reaching way up to an impossibly high ceiling supported by unlikely Ionic columns—the simple, high-tech, right out of the industrial kitchen catalogue fixtures of chromed metal grids with natural wood tops. But,—the effect is riveting. White metal lamps—very institutional—float through the space to bring light down to the marvelous foods—all the casual groupings of coffee bags and produce bushels—all very artistic and artful.

This store opened in 1976 and is already an "institution" for those who know and want gourmet-type food. The artists, the would-be artists and those who can afford to be patrons for the artists wander through this two aisled, 2500 sq. ft. shop in Soho as though it were a museum of food—contemplating and appreciating the "works" before them. It is a gastronomic voyage down the long narrow side aisles with exquisitely prepared foods, mounds of exotic cheeses and olives in glass cases to one side and an infinite variety of carefully selected olive oils, vinegars, spices and seasonings hugging the walls on their metal racks. Baskets hang over the main central food counters and in the rear under an ancient skylight—right out of La Boheme—a vast selection of cooking utensils.

In this old, 19th cent. building, this contemporary food store combines the old with the new—the exquisite with the delicious.

Dean & DeLuca, Prince St., NYC

81

Working within a tight budget, the architects/designers were able to produce this big, open, high-tech gourmet food shop. On the lower level, the assorted foods are presented in "islands" with rounded ends that invite the shopper to move in and around them. The upper level contains food-related items and novelties. The designers sought to combine visual excitement with function. The fixtures are finished in white laminates with a fresh apple green color used as an accent throughout—for that out-of-doors feeling. This scheme allows the food and the packaging to create their own everchanging palette of colors. The duct work is exposed and like the free-form, high-tech staircase it becomes part of the "au courant" design.

A demonstration area is at the far end of the major aisle with an angled mirror above so that shoppers, anywhere in the store, can see what is going on. The lighting is bright and sharp—reflecting off all the white surfaces.

Throughout the floor plan, emphasis was placed on providing display opportunities within the shop.

Russ Vernon is the guiding genius behind the successful 25,000 sq. ft. gourmet shop in Akron. "Our first and foremost function is to be of service to the customer. We want her to feel comfortable in the store." The store was designed with comfort—and convenience—but what is quite extraordinary here is the lighting which won a National lighting award for excellence. Working closely with Russ Vernon and studying customer shopping habits, the designers came up with a new management of aisles and departments—which in turn recommended a subtler use of color, form and light. Each food or display required its own unique lighting; crisp over seafood to enhance the delicate colors and in the wine department a variety of settings would be needed depending upon what use or function might be going on there.

The ceilings were painted dark and also lowered to seven different levels for a more human scale and to break the cavernous feeling of the space. In some departments custom cedar grids were used—in others parabolic diffusers.

Special areas were given special treatment; the wine department, the gourmet chocolate shop, and fruit baskets are assembled on the floor for show, color and the excitement it offers. Posters and paintings were included into the design scheme along with unique, handcrafted wooden fixtures and displayers. Even the restrooms are beautifully illuminated and fresh flowers are added daily. Russ Vernon knows how to make his customers comfortable.

What began as a neighborhod deli in 1939 is now a Gourmet Empire and yet the shop still maintains the look, feel and smell of the deli—only more so. It is unbelievable how much is physically crammed into the 8000 sq. ft. of display space!

Many shoppers are "regulars" coming for their weekly "fix" of scotch salmon that is flown in weekly—or the croissants that are made fresh every twenty minutes. As they did almost fifty years ago, Zabar's still fillets and pickles its own herrings and prepares the sauces in their own kitchens.

Part of the "Zabar Mystique" is the crowd—the swarming of bodies pushing through produce and grocery clogged aisles—past old time "grocery-type" hand scrawled signs,—piles upon piles of provisions, and just barely overhead—cooking utensils, baskets and gift items. There is no uniform "design" or "theme." It is all presentation—visual merchandising—food set up and out on folded cardboard cartons or wooden baskets or bushels —or "antique" milk bottle boxes—or the newer plastic ones.

On the second level, the 5,500 sq. ft. Mezzanine provides a full display of gourmet cookwear. At Zabar's they do "Gourmet" the old-fashioned way—and it works.

D.D.L. Foodshow,
Columbus Ave., NYC
Design: Adam Tihany, NYC

The biggest foodshow in town was up on Columbus Ave. in 12,000 sq. ft. of rehabbed space in the once elegant, now restored Endicott Hotel. Through the windows—the feast began; the freshly baked breadstuffs up against the glass and inside the bakegoods counter and a small sit-down cafe for a coffee or a cappuccino. On the other side of the entrance, you could watch the pasta being rolled, shaped and cut by hand. Stepping inside meant moving into a warm, glowing interior of old brick, gleaming brass, and handsome natural woods. The decorative cast iron columns that were an integral part of the original construction were painted to match the deep blue of the glazed floor tiles interspersed with terra cotta tiles.

The shopper stepped up several steps—passed candy on one side and a glorious wall of brass and copper cannisters, containers, roasters and grinders—and dozens of different aromatic coffee beans. A rhythmic brick arcade separated a series of small specialty food shops and at the end—Valhalla! A sweeping glass barrel vault covered what was originally the Palm Court of the dowager hotel.

89

FOODS AREAS IN DEPARTMENT STORES

The mid nineteenth century saw the advent of the Department Store as we know it today. By that time Dry Goods stores were established sights on Main streets and as the country stretched its frontiers ever westward—so did the itinerant peddler travel with his something-for-everybody wagon into this fertile territory and settle down and open Dry Goods stores with their basic stock. It wasn't long before "staples"—food staples were added on to the Dry Goods shelves; barrels of crackers and pickles added on to the floor—flour, sugar, tea and coffee, and spices—along with fresh baked breads and pies and local produce. ZCMI in Salt Lake City, Utah is considered the oldest department store in the U.S., and when it was established in 1867 it had a food emporium, and its current food area still plays an important part in the store's totality. ZCMI was preceded by the first Parisian department store, the Bon Marche, in the early 1850s though it started out as a dry goods operation in 1838. Harrod's, in London, opened its elegantly tiled and ornamented Food Hall in 1901. Harrod's began as a small grocery store back in 1849 and eventually the Dry Goods were added on to make this one of England's great stores. The store has grown in stature and been expanded and enlarged several times—many product lines have been added —and today these handsome, high-ceilinged, marble countered chambers, where the display of the produce is so exquisite, have become a must-see "sight" for visitors to London.

It has always been a convenience for the department store shopper to find a "gourmet shop"—"A specialty candy shop"—"a catering service"—"a wine area" within the confines of the department store. Mostly the food areas did not replace the market or supermarket for the everyday food staples, but were the place to pick up a gift item, or a special treat. The Japanese depart-

ment stores seemed to change all that in the late 60s and early 70s as they added large food markets—usually on the lower levels—of their in-town stores where the shopper could not only find the "treats" and the "unusual" foods, but also that evening's meal already prepared and portioned—and beautifully presented for the aesthetic eye. The vast subterranean halls were filled with myriad smells eminating from cauldrons—from ovens—off of griddles and charcoal braziers—and from many small, intimate cafes and fast food counters polka dotted over the area providing oases for a quick snack or the instant gratification of the "sweet tooth"—or to soothe a parched throat.

The food departments in the U.S. have, in many cases, grown to include fast food stands, soda fountains, cafes and even restaurants for sit-down-and-relax lunches or dinners. The food is on view; salad bars, buffet tables, steam tables, dessert carts, and the in-store food operations are done with the flair and deft touch the shoppers have come to expect of department store designers, visual merchandisers and the specialists who have been brought in to supervise these all important areas.

In this chapter we visit some European stores as well as several in Japan, and in the United States where the food departments are not just "conveniences" for the customer but are definite "draws" and sometimes the primary reason for the visit to the store. Presentation is important and display plays a major role in making the Food area so successful. The color, lighting, textures and patterns of the design of these areas are coordindated to produce the appealing and appetizing ambience, and the heady aromas bring the shoppers from other levels in the store to where the food is available.

Filene's, Boston, MA
Design: Norwood Oliver Design Assoc., NYC

For Filene's:
Mike Boccadoro, V.P. Store Planning & Design, and staff
Arthur Crispino, V.P. Visual Merchandising.

In traditional downtown Boston we have the redesigned
and revitalized "old-time", traditional setting for specialty
foods and gourmet delights in a department store.

The ceilings are covered with embossed tin sheeting to
recall a past era, and where the wood timbered ceiling is
emphasized we are taken even further back in time. The
floors are wood covered and so is almost everything
else—except those areas that are enhanced with hand
decorated tiles. The warm, polished oak wood is
highlighted with copper and brass and the fixtures, though
contemporary, are showing their "past" with moldings,
glass dome shields and porcelain knobs. The coffee shop
(left) is an excellent example of good store design and
fixturing combined with visual merchandising and display
for a winning combination.

The Macy's Marketplace became an instant success when it opened in the totally renovated basement in the Herald Square store fifteen years ago. The "life-style" concept brought together food, stationary and housewares in one area with individual "shops" off a main piazza for the Macy's regulars—and for the impulse shoppers who work in the area—to shop. It was a special blessing for the thousands of commuters who rush through the store on their way to trains and busses; a "one-stop" shop for dinner—and more.

In the wood filled space the shopper can buy caviar, select tea or coffee from a very large selection, buy prime meats or prepared salads or dishes made according to Macy's own tested recipes, or sample from hundreds of especially imported or domestic cheeses. Chocolates are flown in from Belgium—smoked salmon from Scotland.
The floor is constantly being changed, enhanced and improved to provide the shopper with the most—and the best.

Macy's Celler—The Marketplace, NYC
Joe Cicio, V.P. Macy's Store Planning & Design

Macy's, Riverchase, Hoover, AL
Design: Hambrecht Terrell, NYC
Photo: Charles McGrath

Macy's, Willowbrook
Mall, NJ
Design: Hambrecht
Terrell, NYC
Photo: Ashod
Kassabian

The successful "Cellar" and the "Marketplace" within the Cellar is found in many Macy's stores around the country, —some in the cellar—others up on the second level. There are similarities in each; the traditional wood bases and counters, and white tiled floors often enriched with mosaic inlays,—the hanging, etched glass shades the profusion of foods displayed on feature tables. Plants add to the at-home look of the space.

Louie B's, Macy's, Christiana Mall, DE
Design: Tucci, Segrete and Rosen, NYC

94

Marshall Field, Chicago, IL   Design: Tucci, Segrete and Rosen, NYC

Belk's Charlotte, NC
Design: Hambrecht Terrell International, NY
For Belk's: Cecil Bessellieu, S.V.M.
V.P. Store Planning & Visual Merchandising

Beneath a lowered ceiling, on the lower level, enveloped in a warm, woody interior is the food and gourmet shop within the store. The fixtures are made of wood relieved with high-tech, chromed shelves, and a colorful diamond checkerboard pattern wraps the fascia over the perimeter shops and also appears as pennants out on the floor. The intimate space is warmed by incandescent lights recessed in the ceiling, and the neon signage is easily visible in the selling space. The dining area is tiled and light, and a happy oasis for the shopper who wants a "break". Through the boldly mullioned window one can see the food area and its diamond patterned decor.

Bloomingdales, The Falls, Miami, FL
Design: Hambrecht Terrell, NYC
Photo: Michael Datoli

Here is a sampling of Bloomingdales food sections. The fixtures range from "provincial" to "contemporary,"—from light, bleached woods to deep, rich mahogany. Most have terra cotta tiled floors and, again—depending upon the location,—the textures vary from smooth to country-rough. In some locations natural parquet wood floors are used—or even marble in special food areas. The wall shelf units are well illuminated and the floor fixtures are lit from above. Display plays an important part in the look of the Food Shops at Bloomingdales.

Bloomingdales, King of Prussia, PA   Design: Norwood Oliver Design Assoc., NYC

Bloomingdales, Willow Grove, PA

99

Harrod's, Brompton Rd., London, England
Visual Presentation Director: John Macketrick
Photos: Louis B. Bernstein, NJ

Harrod's began as a small grocery store back in 1849. The shop contained one counter behind which two assistants sold tea, biscuits, soap and candles. Today, Harrod's Food Hall covers more than 46,000 sq. ft. and has become one of the must-see shopping sites in London. The Hall encompasses a bakery, a Wine & Spirit Hall, fruit, vegetables, flowers, meat, fish and poultry. During the many enlargements and renovations of this Hall which dates back to the turn of the century, there has been the addition of brown and green tiles by Malkin and large, dome-topped mirrors in the Bakery. The Royal Doulton Co. was selected to produce the Parian ware tiles which are used in twenty medallions depicting farming and hunting secnes—set in an overall pattern of stylized fishes, birds and trees.

Recently incorporated into the newly added-on areas of the Hall are an extended Health Food department, a flower/food order desk, a permanent cooking demonstration area, a Fruit Tea shop where tasting is encouraged and a handsomely decorated coffee counter. As evident in these views, displays are an integral part of the food presentation at Harrod's.

Harrod's, Brompton Rd., London, England
Visual Presentation Director: John Macketrick
Photos: Louis B. Bernstein, NJ

The Broadway, Costa Mesa, CA   Design: Cole, Martinez & Curtis, Marina Del Rey, CA

Robinson's, Horton Plaza, San Diego, CA   Design: Cole Martinez & Curtis, Marina Del Rey, CA

JWR MARKET

Two well known California department store chains are presented here. Left: The Broadway store is white and light and warm. Large white ceramic square tiles are mixed with natural wood floors and "provincial" display and feature tables. The two Robinson stores, on this page, are also predominantly white. In the restaurant area, the fantastic display of food provides the main thrust of color under the multi-angled, mirrored ceiling. An angled ring of spots lights up the varied display of food in the faceted cases in the center of the area.

Robinson's, Costa Mesa, CA
Design: Hambrecht Terrel, NYC
Photo: Jack Boyd

103

The Daimaru Food Halls in Tokyo and Osaka, Japan

The Japanese department stores are noted for their Food Halls,—usually one or two levels below the main floor entrance, but on the level with the subway and the people rushing to or from work. In addition to the standard and anticipated provisions, the halls are filled with the marvelous aromas of foods being freshly prepared. All is crisp, neat and clean; the salespersons in white smocks and head coverings, kneading, cutting, cooking and baking the foods in full view of the shoppers. Throughout, small cafes and bars are located for sampling or snacking. Incandescent lamps serve as strong highlights in the already brightly lit spaces.

The Daimaru Food Halls in Tokyo and Osaka,
Japan

Mitsokushi, Tokyo, Japan

Seibu, Tokyo, Japan

These Food Halls are as well equipped and provisioned as a super, supermarket—and often more so. At Seibu, above, two expansive floors are devoted to Japanese and International foods, and both traditional regional products and gourmet convenience foods are featured here. They have introduced the Gourmet Express Line of Japanese, Western and Chinese cuisine items designed for quick preparation at home by their time conscious customers. Under the illuminated barrel vaulted ceiling of glass panes, —the shoppers wander down the white tile aisles. Throughout, incandescent lamps are suspended down over the merchandise to make them glow in the warm light.
Left: At Mitsokushi, the fresh fish counters are enhanced by the dropped lights where the food is cut-up and prepared to order.

In the newly revised and devised Strawbridge & Clothier (above) the fast food area has taken a dramatic turn with the food display set in this loft-y area. The counters and floors are patterned in terra cotta, black and deep rust on creamy white, and the checkerboard pattern motif carries through up on the fascia over the service area on the two sides. The high peaked ceiling,—slotted with glass panes, allows light in during the daylight hours. The post-modern/classic elements reappear throughout the store.

Right: At Woodward & Lothrop,—in the newly up-dated and up-scaled store, the food area is bathed in the reflected glow of copper panels, fascias and rails,—played against gray terrazzo floors and baseboards. The feature tables are white enameled and topped with natural wood,—"contemporary-country" in style. This Metro Center Market is the underground entrance that links Woodies with the D.C. mass transit system. As in the Tokyo shops, the potential customers who shop this 4400 sq. ft. food emporium are commuters. Here they can find special blends of coffee, gourmet vinegars, Godiva chocolates,—or pick up prepared foods for lunch—or dinner. The barrel vaulted ceiling reflects the underground setting. The colors are warm and energetic; lighting is indirect with accent highlighting on special merchandise, the menu boards and displays.

108   Strawbridge & Clothier, King of Prussia, PA
Design: Pavlik Design Assoc., FL
Visual Merchandising Director: John Witmeyer

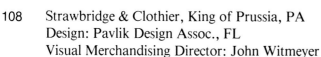

Woodward & Lothrop, Metro Center, Washington, DC
Design: Robert Young Assoc., Alexandria, VA
Visual Merchandising Director: Jack Dorner, V.P.

Though the basement has been there for over eighty years, it has only been during the last few years that "700 Under the Mall" has arisen and taken over as the place to shop—to browse and to sample in busy downtown Minneapolis. Finding the old and making it new again, the architects used the exposed brick foundation as a series of archways that lead to individual "worlds" in this underworld. The food is in the Marketplace which combines the feeling of an open air market with glossy white counters and friendly, wood encased, oak plank floored food shops. Here the shopper finds the Deli, a bakery, a candy shop (far lower right) and a gourmet gift shop (right). There are also some fast food stands, but for a more relaxed meal where food is on display, the shopper goes up to the twelfth floor to the sensuous curves and light, glossy surfaces of the Skyroom designed by J. Holmlund International Ltd. of Minneapolis.

Dayton's, Minneapolis, MN
Design: Tucci, Segrete & Rosen, NYC
For Dayton's: Andrew Markopoulos, S.V.M.
V.P. Store Planning & Visual Merchandising
Charles Z. Kind, V.P. Properties

Dayton's, Minneapolis, MN
Design: Tucci, Segrete & Rosen, NY
Andrew Markopoulos, S.V.M., V.P. of Store
Design/Visual Merchandising

The Woodward Store, Ltd., Vancouver, B.C., Canada
Visual Merchandising Director: J.L. DeBruin, SVM

No! This is not a supermarket! It is a super sophisticated Food Hall in the Woodward Store Ltd. in Vancouver. The lower level of the store is done in red and green in a pre-dominantly white environment—from floor to ceiling. The vegetables and fruits are "characterized" by the green walls, giant graphics and the flattering (to the produce) green enameled fixtures. Cheese, fish and meat products are set out in a red environment. Throughout the wide open and airy space, fabric awnings are used to identify the special shops or areas. The brightly colored, shiny arched awnings are emblazoned with neon script and outlines—to catch the eye and deliver the message to anywhere on the mirror columned floor. In addition to the fluorescents set into the acoustical filed ceiling, track lights are used to accentuate the display presentations.

EAT IN-TAKE OUT

"Would ye both eat your cake and have your cake?"
John Heywood (1497-1580), Proverbs.

You can eat your cake and still have your cake to take home with you from the conditori—the patisserie—the tea room or the bakery-cum-cafe. You can also eat your slice of pizza and still take home another wheel of cheese and tomato sauce,—or pasta salad or any variety of completely prepared ready-to-go-and-eat-later foods, —or just sit down and enjoy some of it at once. It is the retailing miracle of Eat in/Take out, and though many fast food operations are also prepared with plastics to carton-to-go hamburgers, fries, egg-rolls and cokes, in this chapter we are addressing those shops that go beyond "fast foods" and become "respectable" dinner entrees. It often starts with a whiff—an aroma that permeates the premises—that sends messages to the palate and signals the eyes to look,—and what one sees is what one buys. Up front,—an array of beautifully prepared and arranged—and displayed platters filled with tempting morsels that do justice to the smell—sweet or pungent—in the air. How can anyone not want to bite a bit out of a chocolate chip cookie—right now when the rich scent surrounds you and strokes your senses? So while packing up a "pound to go"—you buy one "for the road."

Eat in/Take out in food operations is not new historically but they have reached new heights of sophistication over the last decade or so. They combine the 70s "me" attitude with the early 80s "now" needs and put the emphasis on today's desire to save time—

even if it costs more to save that time. It is convenience—it is comfort—it is knowing in advance, often by on-the-spot taste testing that what you have is right —and will satisfy a later "need." No need for pots and pans—heat in the kitchen—advance planning and preparation. With the miracle of the Micro-Wave—it is ready in minutes—it is fool proof—and you know it.

In this chapter we will see examples of Eat in/Take out in dual operations that satisfy the shopper in a hurry—whether it be a pick-up breakfast of croissants, rolls or Danish and coffee in a conveniently located, downtown bakery/cafe,—or a prepared Pasta shop that comes to meet the commuter on the run from the station to his/her home. We will sample Pizza Parlors that are slick and ambience rich—and where the art of flying pizza dough provides a floor show for those who sit to be served—or those who wait to-go.

In describing the London scene of 1830, William Cobbett wrote in "Rural Rides," "Nowadays all is looked for at the shops. To buy the thing ready-made is the taste of the day. Thousands who are housekeepers buy their dinners ready cooked." Even way back then —at the start of the Industrial Revolution—women who worked all day at the factory didn't have the time—or the energy to cook large meals. Times may have changed but the situation is quite similar—but my how the selection has changed.

Lakeside Deli, Oakland, CA
Design: Ace Architects, Oakland, CA

The architects expanded this traditional Italian-style
delicatessen from a 15 ′ wide by 18 ′ long space into a 30 ′ x
70 ′ area which now also accomodates up to 50 patrons
between the Pantheon-esque rotunda up front (above), the
space in the garden, and on the small mezzanine (left). The
classic Italian influence can be felt in the neo-classic
Pompeiian murals that adorn the walls and the exuberant
waves and crests—and the Triton figure executed in the
terrazzo floor a la a mosaic pavement. A shaft of light
enters through the oculus in the domed ceiling. This
"temple of food" is further enriched with painted garlands
and foliage swags by the artist Joe Ruffuto. In the garden,
real ivy grows up the trellis and the rails that lead to the
rotunda entrance.

Warburton Bakery, Boston, MA
Design: Morris Nathanson Design, Pawtucket, RI
Photos: Warren Jagger, Providence, RI

This page: Warburton's was conceived to be what American's perceive as "English Style"; "old world charm"—a touch of class, and quality products produced and sold here,—and all in a space of about 2000 sq.ft. including the cafe. Soffit signage, mini-tile, checkerboarded floors, painted brick walls covered with framed prints and memorabilia and warm, pleasant light reinforce the image.

Opposite page: Alchemy started out to be a "great take-out bagel shop" but the concept and menu expanded in this 3200 sq.ft. space which accomodates up to 80 patrons. The materials are functional, honest and require minimal maintenance. The food display is the dominant element in the design—assisted by the black/white mosaic floor with pink drop in dots. White tile continues above the beaded wood wainscot and the walls are finished in white, gray and black zolotone under a gray 2x2 suspended ceiling with low voltage track lighting.

Alchemy Ovenworks, Providence, RI
Design: Morris Nathanson Designs, Pawtucket, RI

Opposite Page: C'est Si Bon is "an intimate French Gourment store and restaurant" that specializes in fresh baked French breads and pastries, gourment foods and cheeses. The designers, to please the French owners, had to create a "French" up-scaled look as it might be perceived by the Greenwich patrons. French blue and light woods were mainly used because they suggested "Country French" and French wallpapers, French beech woods with matching laminates, and floor tiles completed the picture. Lighting was used to create warm, intimate spaces in the shop.

This page: A 200 sq.ft. snack shop in what was meant to be an up-scaled, busy shopping center in midtown N.Y. The designer "increased" the space with mirrored walls and almost totally glass cases where fresh baked goods are openly displayed under high intensity lighting. The black and white scheme plus the bright, clear lighting proved very effective, and the graphics supplied the touches of color.

C'est Si Bon, Greenwich, CT
Design: Vinik Assoc., Hartford, CT
Photo: Warren Jagger, Providence, RI

Caffe Luna, Newton, MA
Design: Morris Nathanson Design, Pawtucket, RI

Opposite page: To create a "romantic Northern Italian sidewalk cafe", the designers selected the earthy colors, stucco textures and "frescoes" of Florence plus the black and white tiles of the Duomo in Siena. The imagery of "Luna" called for planetary spheres and faux painted starlit skies. In addition, the shop is filled with arcitectural pilasters and mahogany with accents of teal, maroon and gilt.

This page: In a century old building on a newly up-scaled street in a once run-down area, the architects created this charming oasis that combines the traditional qualities of the structure and the warm, cozy friendly "kitchen" heritage of the baked cakes, pies and breads.

Sarabeth's Kitchen, Amsterdam Ave., NY
Design: Grandesign, NY

American Cafe Market, Tysons Corner, VA
Design: Charles Morris Mount, NY

American Cafe Market,
Capital Hill, Wash. D.C.
Design:
Charles Morris Mount, NY
Photo: Durston Saylor, NY

American Cafe Market, Harborplace, Balt.,MD
Design: Charles Morris Mount, NY
Photo: Norman McGrath, NY

A chain of fine food-shops-cum-cafes is centered in
the Washington, D.C., Virginia and Maryland
area—mostly in up-scaled malls, and the shops present a
bright, contemporary image in their tile wrapped interiors.
The lighting is warm as are the colors used in the shops
and the food display is a major consideration in the overall
layout and design of the spaces. The signage and
graphics—plus the displays add to the clean, inviting
interiors.

American Cafe Market, Fair Oaks, VA
Design: Charles Morris Mount, NY

Connie's Pizza, Chicago, IL
Design: Donahue Designs, Chicago, IL
Architect: R.L. Winfield Wood, Arlington Hgts. IL

The architect created an all new "old" turn-of-the-century warehouse to encase this 15000 sq.ft. enterprise. The designer "staged" an imaginary wholesale market—as it might have looked then—where Italian restauranteurs would buy produce and imported oils, cheeses and spices. Each "storage area" becomes a dining space with movable shelving partitions to accomodate small, private parties. Half of the entire space is devoted to the kitchen which produces 1000 Chicago-style pizzaz daily. Architectural details create the interior warehouse look; the floor is constructed of 6″ wood, center cut grain planks and there are lots of beams, columns and exposed brickwork, wine presses, barrels, displays of food products, storage bins and more.

Connie's Pizza, Chicago, IL
Design: Donahue Designs, Chicago, IL
Architect: R.L. Winfield Wood, Arlington Hgts. IL

La Boulangerie, NY
Design: Charles Morris Mount, NYC
Photo: Durston Saylor

Above: In a long, narrow space the designers created a functional French Bakery, Espresso Bar and Charcuterie. They broke the space up into three zones that are visually and physically related to each other. Mirrored walls attract the pedestrians and sanded glass lamps lower the ceiling line. Opaline sconces with crystal ornamentation adorn the wall of mirrors. All the cabinetry is curved to create a sinuous traffic flow. In European tradition, the espresso bar is marble—with mirrors abounding. Low voltage spots enhance the food and the blue-gray color adds to the sophistication, while the light turquoise glass tiles add brightness and elegance to the atmosphere. Colored soffits help define the spaces.

Right: The key to designing the 2500 sq. ft. deli and food bar, Pasta & Co. is the lavish display of prepared gourmet foods. The company began with just the sale of food, but this new shop includes sit-down service. The curved glass display case is prominently set down at the entrance. The distinctive black/white/yellow color scheme is highlighted with brass. A checkerboard pattern is used on the floor—on the logo (seen on the menu board)—and the yellow lunch bags that are used for carry-out and delivery service. Shelves are surfaced in brass and brass inserts are set into the marble floor. Yellow plaster board panels are suspended from the black ceiling to focus the eye on the products below.

Pasta & Co., Seattle, WA
Design: Retail Concepts of the NBBJ Group
Seattle, WA
Photo: Paul Warchol

Fat Apples, El Cerruto, CA
Design: David Baker, Arch., Berkley, CA

French Bakery, Claypool Court, Indianapolis, IN
Melvin Simon Development

Above: Fat Apples restaurant & bakery is located in a rehabbed 6000 sq. ft. supermarket building. The hanger-like interior is treated "as a generic volume within which the large oven, the managers office and mezzanine buildings form a city under the sky vault of exposed wood ceiling and clean span barrel vaulted trusses." Operationable skylights "daylight" the building.

The French bakery is bright and colorful due to the extensive use of colored graphics over the service area and the canvas banners that angle across the narrow shop.

The Chicken Nest (right top) is traditional in its wood cabinetry and the white tile flooring.

Popeye goes for an even more "traditional," turn-of-the-century, "good old days" ambience with Victorian wood working, turnings and details. The colored glass valance, over the central area, and the embossed "tin" ceiling complete the look. For good measure, the designers added "gas lamp" chandeliers and ceiling fans—all to complement the old style, Southern style, fried chicken—Cajun style.

128

Chicken Nest, Livingston, NJ
Design: Dorf Associates, NYC

Popeye Fried Chicken, New Orleans, LA

FAST FOODS

If you were to visit Pompeii today, the guide on the tour would point out the McDonalds of that classic Roman period. You will have to fill in some of the details, but there is still lots left to show that fast foods were an important part of that civilized and sophisticated City's everyday lifestyle. There is a counter, though the stools are gone. There are service areas; a deep concavity that, two thousand years ago contained the "hot soup de jour"—and another for the featured "plate" of the day. As you look around this early fast food operation, you can still see traces of the murals that decorated the walls,—of carved ornaments and moldings that enriched the walls—and mosaic floors with taste-tempting subjects. Not too far from the "cafe" is the remains of the oven where the aroma of the freshly baked loaves must have sent up smell signals to the unsuspecting Romans on the rutted street.

The street vendors and pastry cooks at the markets and fairs brough the "fast foods" to the customers. They went where the shopper was and supplied instant gratification—instant pleasure—satisfying hunger or just pleasing the palate. At the Roman Baths, slaves circulated through the halls selling refreshments; cakes, sausages, lettuce, eggs and lizard fish. In 18th century European cities, orange vendors filled the theaters in London and Paris, supplying the audience with a thirst-quenching snack—or ammunition to pelt the unfortunate actors. In 1765, M. Boulanger started his catering career as a soup seller. He called his soups

"Restaurants"—restoratives. He went on to become famous for his sheep's feet in white sauce.

Today, food is still coming to the shopper whether it is a falafel stand on wheels in Jerusalem—a spring roll cart in Hong Kong—a taco vendor in Guadalajara or the aluminum frankfurter wagon complete with fringed umbrella on the streets of N.Y. It can be a bus or a van by the side of a busy road that dishes out the prepared delicacies. Fast food establishments have done just that—come off wheels and established "roots" in Food Courts in malls—in department stores where they serve the shopper and also the store by keeping the shopper in the store. The stands or shops are designed to complement the food—by color—texture—or decorative motifs—to suggest something about the food (ethnicity—taste—fun) and to satisfy the customer's comfort.

In this chapter we will highlight some of today's Fast Food operations,—in malls—in centers—in railroads and airports—in department stores and free standing in town or on the highway. There are thematic concepts and historic designs, but whatever the sources for architecture and decoration, the "star" is still the food and the presentation of that food—Up Front—under lights—backed up with the right colors—pleasing textures—that enhance the product. The ambience must be appealing and satisfying—and add to the pleasure of the dining experience, but the "come-on"—the lure—the attraction—is still the food up front.

Fruit Works, Mall at Mill Creek, Secaucus, NJ
Design: Q-5, Wayne, NJ

Bananas, Garden State Mall, Paramus, NJ
Design: Q-5, Wayne, NJ

It's Only Natural, Mall at Mill Creek, Secaucus, NJ
Design: Q-5, Wayne, NJ

Dimitrio's, Columbus, OH   Design: Linda Danjell Designs, Columbus, OH   Photos: Jeff Rycus

Left: Dimitrio's is only 1600 sq. ft. and seats 60. The color scheme of this Memphis-inspired design includes red and yellows (popular in fast food operations) plus turquoise for touches of the Mediterranean,—with lots of black and white for sophistication. This is a total package design that includes the cups, napkins, and graphics. The columns are fabric-wrapped for graphic impact and they add to the illusion of depth in the space. The lighting plan includes high intensity projector lamps and small decorative fixtures—in addition to canisters on tracks. The bold graphics and strong colors under the sharp light draw the mall shoppers into Dimitrios.

Figaro is also predominantly black, white and red—with a contemporary/classic leaning. It is a "landscape of archtypes; obelisks, Palladian walls, the Italian flag, white chairs and tables—"all in a long, narrow space replicated infinitely in the two, large facing mirrors—creating a Piazza out of the small shop with 720 sq. ft. storefront. Galvanized steel spiral columns with shell metal lintels and pilasters frame the entrance arcade. The up-front serving counter is topped by a menu-board of red, white and green acrylic. The architect describes this store as a "giant cappuccino machine all shiny, bright and gleaming"— like in traditional coffee bars in Italy.

Figaro, Oakland, CA
Design: Ace Architects, Oakland, CA
Photo: Rob Super

McDonald's is much more than a hamburger. Right: the 5000 sq. ft. operation at Rockefeller Center is based, in spirit, on the art deco of its surroundings. The "unexpected" palette includes blue, gray, and salmon reinforced with stainless steel, ceramic tiles and matching plastic laminates. The tile aisles create a fast, decorative traffic flow pattern. Large expanses of mirrored walls seem to stretch the width of the narrow space and channels of stainless steel add texture to the walls—and the mirrors. Two bands of electric blue neon outline the sinuously curved drop ceiling and theatrical lighting tends to up-scale the ambience of this store.

The Paramus Park McDonald's is dominated by the warm, rosy-pink color of the floor tiles, walls, seat covering, table tops and ceiling. The cool refreshing accent is the blue glow emanating from the glass block columns that figure predominantly on the floor,—and that is reflected in the copper bands that outline the wall panels and contain the glass column enclosures. Incandescent lamps add to the warmth and glow of the operation as do the half-bowl up lights that act as wall sconces.

McDonalds, Paramus Park, NJ
Design: Charles Morris Mount, NYC
Photos: Norman McGrath

McDonalds, Rockefeller Center, NYC
Design: Charles Morris Mount, NYC
Photo: Norman McGrath

Far Right: Cravings by Forte is a modern dessert and late snack restaurant. Visual display of the desserts and ice-cream—as well as the final preparation of the cake decorating reinforce the take-home/catering areas. All the design elements are ultra modern, ultra sophisticated and avant-garde but the matte black mixed with white, gray, mauve-pink, and faux copper glass displays soften the sharp, linear look. The lattice screens are a decorative motif that are used on the walls—as dividers—and frames on the windows that look down onto the street below. Display type low voltage lighting adds a theatrical ambience to the restaurant.

In a speed-oriented location—at a busy airport—Fast Lane takes on the sweep and feeling of an air current at take off. The same sweep of the drop ceiling follows through into the sitting space which is all gray, black and white with accents of "sky-blue" light. The square dot motif connects the fast food stalls with the dining areas in an unselfconscious manner.

Fast Lane, O'Hare Airport, Chicago, IL
Design: Green, Hiltscher, Shapiro, Ltd. Arch.
Chicago, IL
Photos: Barry Rustin

Cravings by Forte, Toronto, Ont., Canada
Design: Yabu-Pushelberg, Toronto, Ont., Canada
Photos: Shin Sugino

Cafe Milano, U. of CA, Berkley, CA
Design: David Baker, Architect,
Berkley, CA

Left: Cody's occupies a double height space behind a glass bay. The curved white "piano" shaped mezzanine is supported on ebonized wood "piano-legs" which also serve as torchere light fixtures. Up front, the warm-welcoming aroma of fresh breads and Danish.

Cafe Milano, above, is a renovated brick warehouse that was constructed at the turn-of-the-century. The surfaces were stripped back to reveal the original textures and building techniques. Over the complex texture of the revealed concrete floor the designers imposed a grid of black saw cuts of city sidewalk scoring. The original structural column and girder line was defined as a colonnade by painting it silver. The "wall" that slices through the main floor from the sidewalk entrance—to the stairs—to the mezzanine in the rear suggests a building facade—bringing the out-of-doors inside. The street level is filled with plantings and trees.

Cafe Cirque, built in the Indianapolis Union Station is dominated by a mauve and hot pink color scheme—lots of white and a theater marquee of a bygone era—bright colors, neon tubes and running lights. HID lights provide the general lighting but the sitting area is enhanced by the low hung metal shaded lamps.

Cafe Cirque, Indianapolis, IN
Design: Rowland Assoc., Indianapolis, IN
Photo: Elliot Fine, NYC

Cafe Cody, Berkley, CA
Design: David Baker, Architect, Berkley, CA

Mama Mia! Pasta, Chicago, IL
Design: Banks and Eakins, Chicago, IL

The Greenery, St. Vincent's Medical Cntr.,
Toledo, OH
Design: Norris Nathanson Designs, Pawtucket, RI
Photo: Warren Jagger

Left: Mama Mia! Pasta is located in the Chicago
Mercantile Exchange Center—near the river that provided
the inspiration for this contemporary operation.
Interpreting the river's movement is the sweeping ceiling
that undulates and billows its way over the seating area.
The red columns reflect the "classic" influence of Italian

heritage that is also seen in the color scheme of red, white
and green. The crisp white tile floor delineates the traffic
pattern. Mirrors provide reflective surfaces and red neon
tubes reinforce the billows in the "flowing" ceiling.

The Greenery (above) is aglow in red neon reflections off
the highly reflective ceiling. Gray is used with salmon and
dubonnet to create a warm, relaxing interior—a different
feeling from the hospital it is part of. Here everybody
glows with good health—and appetites are sated in the
happy setting.

Chinatown Express, Seventh Ave., NYC
Design: Charles Morris Mount, NYC
Photo: Norman McGrath

Le Wok, Les Halles D'Anjou, Montreal, Que.,
Canada
Design: Optima Design, Montreal, Que., Canada

There is nothing more "American" than Chinese
Food—when it comes to Fast Food dining—and take out.
The Chinatown Express (left) is a slick, shiny, black and
chrome operation—from the black ceramic tiled walls and
counters to the laminate tops and tables. Up front, upon
entering—and inviting display of foods—ready to go or to
be enjoyed in the bright, new setting.

Up in Canada, a more subtle approach in the gray tinted
wood paneling, black/gray/white tiles and accessories. In a
different mall situation, Manchu Wok depends upon the
bright bands of neon against a bright red back wall to
stand out from the surrounding food stalls. The balance of
the stand is white ceramic tiles accented with smaller black
ones.

Manchu Wok, Claypoole Court, Indianapolis, IN
A Melvin Simon development

143

Burger Boy, South St. Seaport, NYC
Design: Dorf Associates, NYC

Mickey's Great American Eatery, Plattsburgh, NY
Design: Dorf Associates, NYC

N.Y. Fries, South St. Seaport, NYC
Design: Dorf Associates, NYC

A variety of fast food operations;—all rich, warm and rewarding. Burger Boy and N.Y. Fries are both located in the hectic third level of the South Street Seaport in NYC and must compete in the noisy hustle and bustle of the food filled floor. Each becomes an oasis of peace—and finesse. Burger Boy is warmed up with lots of oak wood, brick textures and faience terra cotta tiles—with red neon accents. Up front, prepared foods in the self illuminated counter. The N.Y. Fries pink laminate covered stand is enriched and distinguished by a massive oak bullnose trim.

The all laminate and tile Mickey's (far left) is flushed with the glow of salmon laminates—brass tubing and red neon outlining the saw-tooth soffit. Orange Julius combines the "fruit cart" with fresh fruits—up front—with the wood veneered counters,—all with a striped canvas overhead that serves as a fascia—and unifies the stand. "Old Fashioned" cliches are given a new expression—and make a fresh appeal to a new audience.

Orange Julius, So. Lake Mall, Merrivale, IN
Design: Babcock & Schmidt, Bath, OH
Photo: Jim Maguire, Akron, OH

146

Le Jardin Culinaire, Faubourge Ste. Catherine,
Montreal, Que., Canada
Design: Optima Design, Montreal, Que., Canada

Bloomers Ice Cream, Appleton, WI
Design: Myklebust Brockman, Assoc., LaCrosse, WI
Photo: Roger Grant, The Critical Eye

Healthfoods and salads—the new and strong entry in the fast food market that calls for fresh, clean, "healthy" environments. The Healthworks prototype store (upper left) combines natural materials with industrial fixtures in a completely integrated graphics system that includes changeable menu boards and environmental, wall-size photomurals. The color scheme is red, green—lots of white and a plentitude of green plants.

Jardin Culinaire puts the emphasis on the "garden" with the cool, neutral gray-blue tiles with white that complement the salads—and the seafood dishes.

Bloomers Ice Cream is also gray-blue trimmed, in this case, with deep blue—all under soft, low lights that make the neon signage stand out even more.

Lucky's Diner, Woodfield Mall, Shuamberg, IL
Developer: Taubman Co.

Fuddruckers, Clearlake (Houston), TX
Designed by: Ideation; Paul Yarmoulk & Cynthia Turner
Concept: Paul Yarmouth Design: Cynthia Turner

Legal Sea Foods, Burlington Mall, Burlington, MA
Design: Morris Nathanson Designs, Pawtucket, RI
Photo: Warren Jagger

Sea Food "Houses" that combine "old-time" flavor with today's conveniences. Up front, at Legal Sea Food, in a white/gray tiled environment, the fresh sea food is displayed on ice, in refrigerated counters. Etched glass lampshades and blackboards framed in oak continue the "old time" look. The main sitting room retains the turn-of-the-century ambience with the ridged glass lamps, the checkered table cloths and the profusion of palm plants—in the white tile and dark wood setting.

Far Right: Famous Atlantic Fish is another New England Sea Food operation with a strong, traditional, New England look—so dear to their up-scaled suburban Boston diners. Wood walls enriched with moldings, mullioned windows and checkered table cloths set the "look." Small tiles set in a dotted pattern with bordered designs cover the floor. Brass accents, bentwood chairs and milk glass ceiling fixtures all contribute to the nostalgia—and the ambience.

Famous Atlantic Fish Co.,
Chestnut Hill Mall, Newton, MA
Design: Morris Nathanson Design,
Pawtucket, RI
Photo: Warren Jagger

FOOD COURTS

"It is part of a wise man to feed himself with moderate pleasant food and drink—and to take pleasure with perfumes, with the beauty of growing plants, dress, music, sports and theatre—and other places of this kind which man may use without any hurt to his fellows.
Benedict Spinoza, "Ethics" 1632-1677

The Food Court has become the new Community Center—the "downtown" of the suburban communities—the "food and entertainment" draw that brings thousands of auto-mobile people into shopping malls,—into rehabbed mills and fixed-up railroad stations—into theme parks and multi-use super structures. The Food Court has also revitalized the "in-town" shopping center/mall—or multi-purpose building by bringing in thousands of "tired, hungry, yearning to be fed" downtowners who can now eat and shop in the same controlled environment during lunch hours and after the work day ends.

The Food Court has become more than a convenient cluster of fast food counters dishing up the same fast foods under slightly different guises or garnishes. In many malls and centers, the food area has truly become an oasis—a wonderous place of refreshment for the body and the spirit. Exotic plants grow in profusion,—flowers bloom all year round often changing with the seasons,—music fills the air along with the pungent aromas of familiar and unfamiliar spices. The foods are often as exotic as the palm trees that surround the fountain—or sit under the skylight—or the soaring sculptures that add to the gracious ambience of the food court. It is more than hamburgers and fried chicken; it is a smorgesbord of lip smacking, finger-licking, delicacies from Japan, Jamaica, India, China, Greece, Mexico—and more. There is freshly brewed coffees with dozens of unusual flavors and scents,—myriad selections of tea,—and for the "diet conscious" or "health nuts"—assorted salads, fruits, and yogurt dishes and treats. Truly, the Food Court often has something for everyone and also can satisfy all the senses.

The Food Court is the place to sit and see— and be seen. It is the place to rest one's weary feet while refreshing the inner emptiness,—to listen to the music or to listen in on others' conversations and be part of a live soap-opera episode. The "fashion parade" goes on endlessly;it is the place to see who is wearing what, and by checking out the bags and boxes—find out who is buying what and where. It is uncanny to realize that over 300 years ago Benedict Spinoza so well described a phenomenon that wouldn't really appear until centuries later. The court has become the place of "growing plants"—"Where man" (and woman, teenager, and child) can take "pleasure with the 'perfumes'" of foreign foods and seasonings blended with the scents of "Opium," "Passion," "Chanel" and "Lauren." "Music, Sports and Theatre" are often part of the scene—maybe over to a side but definitely part of the view. Some courts have a rather unique vista; an ice-skating rink, a "riverview," a "skyview"—and the marquees of the multiplex movie house snuggling in close to get those who have been fed or yield up those who want to be fed. And, in these troubled times of uncertainty and suspicion, isn't it wonderful that there are still places "which man may use without any hurt to (or by) his fellows" and enjoy the companionship of others in comparative peace—surrounded by the good things in life presented in a happy, relaxing and sense-satisfying environment.

Alexandria Mall, Alexandria, LA
Developer: Herring Marathon Group, Dallas, TX
Architect: Architecture + ,Dallas, TX

153

Food, Etc., Valencia, CA
Design: Interior Spaces, Venice, CA
Architects: Rivers & Christian
Photos: David Glomb

The high volume, fast food operation at the Six Flags
Magic Mountain amusement park bursts with energetic
primary colors—right off a Piet Mondrian palette. Color is
what makes this 10,000 sq. ft. area of fast food stands
work—along with the fun use of high-tech materials that
are used with panache. The existing rafters were painted
white as were the supporting columns. The ductwork,
chairs, tables and benches were repainted and reuphol-
stered in red, yellow and blue. The counters were also
refaced in the same primary color scheme,—backed up
with ceramic tile walls. To hold the explosive colors from
running rampant, the floor is gray accented with the
primaries and the chain link fences that separate and also
serve to direct traffic are painted with the same, bright
colors. Neon signage adds to the festivities. Another
remarkable feature of this extensive renovation of an
existing food court was that it was accomplished for only
$275,000.

154

Right: The two story food court is located inside the 1.3 million sq. ft. Metro Centre and it houses 12 eating establishments. The designers created this 28,000 sq. ft. court where each operation has its own definitive look and style. The central focus of the court is the giant clock that gives the court its name—and theme. The mural behind sweeps night into day and the management invites the shoppers to be entertained by the bugle fanfare, steam whistles, bells and cymbals that sound off before each hour—and the gong for the half hour. The entertainment includes watching the assorted movement of ratchets, pendulums, and a giant metronome.

Clockworks Food Court, Gateshead, England
Design: Hamill & McKinney, Dallas, TX

Indianapolis Union Station, Indianapolis, IN
Design: Rowland Assoc., Indianapolis, IN
Photos: Elliot Fine

Union Station, Dallas, TX

Union Station, St. Louis, MO
Arch: Hellmuth, Obata & Kassabaum, Inc., St. Louis, MO

Some of the major recipients of the TLC sweep of "rehabbing" that is sweeping the country are the long neglected, often under or unused decaying railroad stations that were once proud, elegant spaces,—rich in design and detail—reflecting a more gracious time when they welcomed travelers. Here we present only three of the many that have been converted into "malls" or the food courts of malls. In each instance the original structures with soaring, glazed ceilings and cast iron structural elements have been preserved and original look has been retained. Far Left: The Trackside Market food court is located on the elevated level that once was used by the trains. Though the individual food concessions all have different facades, they maintain a visual harmony that suits the structure. Instead of the original train tracks, slate and quarry tiles recreate the familiar pattern. Below, the Pancake House located on this level.

Under the cast iron columns and girders of the St. Louis Union Station—the food court crowd collects to dine on fast foods in the bright open area. The Dallas Union Station's waiting room—on the second level is handsome and elegant—looking again as it once did long ago—but serving new travelers as a food court.

Genesess Valley Mall, Flint, MI

Wiregrass Commons, Dothan, AL
Developer: Jim Wilson & Assos., Montgomery, AL
Architect: Hellmoth, Obata & Kassebaum
Los Angelas, CA

An elevated central aisle—open and spacious—sets the feeling for Pavilion, and the lowered ceilings, supported by the unusual "spindle" columns provide a sense of intimacy and warmth for the food shops and seating areas beneath the ceilings. Gray and white ceramic tile "barriers" separate the aisle from the major seating areas and the cool light over the aisle contrasts with the warm lighting under the lowered ceilings for a sense of comfort in the food experience.

Right: The Four Seasons Mall also has a Pavilion food court—up on its third level. It is 24,000 sq. ft. with two main aisles that run through the space from front to back. Skylights float over the court and two foundations add to the ambience along with the wrought iron "gazebos."

Pavilion, Valley River Center, Eugene, OR
Arch: Kober, Sclater, Seattle, WA

THE
FOOD
FAIR

TO THE
FOOD FAIR

Southland Mall, Hayward, CA
Design: T.L. Horton Design, Inc., Dallas, TX
Photos: Joe Aker

The designers created the identity—the Food Fair; 16'
archways,—a 150 foot sculptured metal "ribbon" that
wraps around the wall,—a series of floating food mobiles
cut out of foamboard and 8' tall—and many planters filled
with plants and seasonal blossoms. Also—to add
excitement—and pizzazz—to the lower level food court;
brightly colored canvas banners, technicolored umbrellas
and a rainbow of canvas ceiling drops were incorporated
into the space. The candy-striped ribbon is visible, in the
upper photo, through the trees. With the "ribbon" there is
a marquee to announce the staged events in the mall.

165

Newport Mall, Jersey City, NJ

Two New Jersey Malls—one just across the river from NYC. Daylight filters into both food courts on the uppermost levels of these open, steel spanned structures filled with metal trellises and skylights. White is the predominant color in both for the metal structural elements, chairs and tables, even the fronts of the food stands. At Newport Mall, colored tiles and neon rondels provide the distinguishing elements for the food shops. A stepped up area,—under the skylight, becomes a plant filled oasis for quiet eating.

The Campus at Bridgewater Commons (far right) also has neon signage but the design has a more "countrified" look with fan trellis arches and wood benches that envelop the columns. Adding to the "provincial" feeling—the potted plants that become the "capitol" of the columns and the wood slat "awnings" that float between the columns and "lower" the ceiling without cutting out the light.

Bridgewater Commons, Summerville, NJ   Design: Fober-Belluschi   Photos: Alan Weitz/Jeff Aranita

Les Terraces (upstairs) & Courtlands (downstairs),
Metro Centre, North East England
Design: International Design Group, Toronto,
Canada

A different kind of food court with Bistro-type fast food
units on two levels. On the lower level, the diners sit under
large white umbrellas at tables set out on the marble
floor—surrounded by trees and plants—in the well of the
atrium. Bistros are set up in the corners of the open space
(see above) and the food is prepared off the premises and
served to the diners at the tables. The menus are, of
necessity, limited. The upper level (left) is more classic in
feeling and also more intimate in its use of space. Here
too, the cafes are strategically placed on the floor and the
umbrellas are green and white.

Forty Second St. Food Court, NYC   Design: Charles Morris Mount, NYC   Photos: Scott Frances

Left: A food court without the mall,—just a food court located on a lively trafficed street in NYC. The challenge was to create an exciting and desirable space out of a typical narrow city lot—at street level and a basement. Part of the solution was to have the food vendors at street level and place the common eating area downstairs.

At street level, a curving soffit was established to carry the signage and provide a visual line to draw the shopper around the space. Incandescent downlights were used to assure a warm, inviting feeling. Over the counters, pure white light supplied by low voltage halogen fixtures were installed so that the food color was true. Mirrors were used to "widen" the space and vinyl wallcoverings were selected for ease of maintenance. Hard ceramic tiles in "bright bubble gum" colors were selected for the floors. An illuminated glass block partition leads to the entrance of the dining area—down the stairs.

Since there were no windows, a mural provides the outdoors feeling with a southwest mesa interpreted in warm, glowing colors under the vaulted sky-blue ceiling—lit with neon to produce a daylight haze. The vast space created by this painted vista is a "juxtaposition of the cramped confines of the canyons of N.Y." The same colored tiles—in a different pattern are used on the floor. The oak benches work well with the molded plastic chairs and the Formica table tops with rubber edges.

National Place, Washington, DC
Design: Walker Group/CNI, NYC

In the heart of the city—in a totally urban environment, the designers created the food court to comfortably fit in with the sophisticated surroundings. Round columns and elegant ceiling articulation unify the various areas of the indoor mall along with the logo "star" motif, brass signage and directionals. In the food court, the star motif is restated along with the brass tubing that carries rows of incandescent bulbs that not only warmly illuminate the area but make a dazzling, decorative pattern. Neon is used for concession signage and dropped milk glass shades add more warm light over the food presentations.

171

Sun Deck, Pompano Square,
Pompano Beach, FL
Design: Walk Group/CNI, NYC
Photos: Kate Zari/Smith Ariel

Ross Park Mall, Pittsburgh, PA
A Melvin Simon Co. development

Left: The 20,000 sq. ft. second level of offices was converted into the Sun Deck food court by the architects. It was to contain twelve fast food concessions and also provide seating for up to four hundred. The designers added skylights over this mezzanine to bring in the daylight and the rest of the transformation was achieved with Italian porcelain ceramic tile flooring, banquettes of white color-core laminates and the common walls were clad in aqua and white horizontal, color-core bands. Capsule shaped panels with white neon bands identifies the vendors—and the foods being served. The Floridian Tropical theme is continued through the use of pink and aqua pastels in bold patterns—and with the foliage.

Jacksonville Landing, Jacksonville, FL   Arch: Benj. Thompson & Assoc., Cambridge, MA   A Rouse Co. development

Bayside, Miami, FL
Design: Benj. Thompson & Assoc., Cambridge, MA
A Rouse Co. development

It is Festival Time! It's time for fun—frolic and FOOD. The Festival Market theme is presented here in two of its many faces. At Jacksonville Landing (far left) it is a giant marketplace that is as fine and fancy as any department store food area; red ceramic brick paved floors under a red ceiling grid that carries dozens of metal lamp shaded bulbs to illuminate the space. Surrouding the market are fast food concessions and places to eat. Here, you can eat your cake—and still have it.

At Bayside, the second level incorporates the food vendors and the common seating area along with a magnificent view of the bay. The imaginative neon signs on the main level arcade are more than matched by the clever, three-dimensional—and amusing signs on the upper level. At Bayside, every day is a holiday and the ongoing celebration is the food served in the food court.

Two new malls, located only a few short streets from each other in downtown Montreal; one on and one just off Ste. Catherine St. W. The total sleek sophistication of Les Cours Mont Real goes with the "designer" quality shops and the floor above, and the shoppers have an open view into the smart black/white dining space and fast food cafes —from any level in the atrium. Soft lighting illuminates the dining space—white malls and massive round columns reaching up into black wells above,— gray terrazzo floors and light, handsome contemporary chairs and tables for easy maintenance.

Still up-scale, but with a more popular approach is the food court at Place Montreal Trust—on the lower level also. Plants, fountains, and color add to the warmth and excitement of this eating environment where the food concessions with foods of many ethnic types ring the seating space that is open to the light that filters down from the skylights four stories above.

Les Cours Mont Real, Montreal, Que., Canada
Design: Yabu-Pushelberg, Toronto, Ont., Canada
Photos: David Whittaker

Place Montreal Trust, Montreal, Que., Canada
A Cadillac Fairview of Canada development

Liberty Square, Ann Arbor, MI
Design: Jon Greenberg Associates, Berkley, MI

A quick, cross-country sampler of new and different food courts—from N.Y.—the midwest—out to California; hightech—post-modern—contemporary and even shades of the Crystal Palace of another century. Some favor neon signage—others eschew it, but where the common dining area is you are sure to find the soft illumination of incandescent lamps and flattering fixtures. Another standard "fixture" is the foliage—the flowering plants—the shrubs and ofttime trees that fill these indoor-outdoor patios. The tile floors can be elegantly subtle in color or patterned for a gay and happy effect—and there is often a subtle definition between where the food is purchased and where it is eaten. That definition is sometimes made by the flooring pattern,—planters and/or barriers,—or the lighting. The look and feel of the food court is an extension of the look, feel and attitude of the containing mall.

Owings Mills, Baltimore County, MD
Arch: RTML Assoc., Baltimore, MD

Montclair Plaza, Montclair, CA   Design: The Jerde Partnership, Los Angeles, CA

The Courtyard, Aviation Mall, Glenn Falls, NY
Design: Myklebust Brockman, Assoc., La Crosse,
MI
Photo: Rick Campas

Rivercenter, San Antonio, TX

New and exciting and as fun-filled as the Riverwalk area it abuts is the food court at Rivercenter in historic downtown San Antonio. It is part of the glass enclosed mall with a grand view of the narrow meandering "river"—the fountains—trees and plantings and myriad banners in a rainbow of colors. Within, metal corrugated fans fill the ceiling and tend to lower it over the tables and chairs that look so Spanish Mission. The food court is filled with memories of its Spanish (or Mexican) association; the faience tiled floors, the terra cotta planters that are everywhere and the rich, earthy palette of coral, pink, peach and sienna. The food concessions make a bold sweep around the wide arc of the mall space, while the smaller inner arc is an all glass look out onto the river and the terrace outside with additional tables set out under green canvas umbrellas. Hidden between the pleated fans on the ceiling are the lights to warm up an already warm interior. Additional light comes from the milk glass fixtures that bracket off the columns on the floor. The fountains in front, near the windows, brings the river right into the food court.

Northstar Mall, San Antonio, TX

West End Marketplace, Dallas, TX

More Texas food-courts. Far Left: Northstar Mall, also in San Antonio, has recently been up-dated and up-scaled, and the new look is apparent in the newly created food court up on the second level. The main seating area is under a giant skylight which is outlined with incandescent lamps. The same lamps make an attractive border over the food concessions. A fascinating and colorful array of canvas banners in red and yellow divide and lower the ceiling into dimensional coffers. Oak benches, chairs and tables are set out on the multi toned red/terra cotta tiled floor.

For fun—Texas style—it's the rehabbed old warehouse now called The West End Marketplace in the historic section of downtown Dallas. Up on the fourth level— under the old skylight filled roof—held up by heavy wood timber beams are the "wild & wooly" food concessions. The real entertainment—people watching—is accomplished by having the dining counter circling round the open atrium and the diners—on stools—sit facing the opening and the ever changing action on the levels below and the criss-crossing escalators bringing new hungry customers up.

The Promenade, Vaughan, Ont., Canada
Developed by: Cadillac Fairview Corp., Ltd.,
Toronto, Ont, Canada
Architect: R.T.K.T. Associates/Crang & Boake,
Toronto, Ont, Canada

St. James Market, Suburban Sq., Ardmore, PA
Architect: D.I. Architecture, Inc.,Baltimore, MD

Town East Mall, Wichita, KS
Architect: D.I. Architecture, Inc., Baltimore, MD

South Towne Mall, Sandy, Utah
Arch: Kober/Sclater Arch., Seattle, WA
Developer: Koch-Collier Partnership, Salt Lake City,
Utah

Opposite page: Under double glazed skylights and
colorful floating canvas umbrellas is the new, ten tenant
food court in the recently enlarged mall. The light, bright
open area is embellished with live trees growing out of the
beige tile flooring under myriad spots set into the steel
structure of the ceiling.

This page: High tech corrugated metal sheeting and a
skylight system of tinted glazed paneling set 10 ′ apart,
suggests a modern-day version of the old railroad
enclosures of the time when east met west in the late
1800s—near this very mall. Granite tiles are used on the
floor and the structural arch motif further reinforces the
railroad imagery. Fourteen food tenants provide the
refreshments in this double arcaded space.

Town Center at Cobb, Cobb County, GA
Arch: RTKL Assoc., Baltimore, MD
Developer: Cadillac Fairview, White Plains, NY

Promenade at Pacific Beach, Pacific Beach, CA
Arch: SGPA Planning & Architecture, San Diego, CA
Developer: Trammell Crow Co., Dallas, TX

This page: Four restaurants anchor this complex
and the food court is located on the second level with a
centralized area. In keeping with the location, the
architecture invites the outside in through open stuccoed
arches and an umbrella ceiling of herrinbone planks of
wood. The floors are covered with natural terra-cotta tile
blocks.

Opposite page: A steep pitched glass and steel roof allows
in the daylight in this up-to-date basilica-styled food area.
The arcades divide the space into a central dining garden
with the food stalls located along the two side aisles. The
color palette is cool with aquamarine and sea green
predominating.

INDEX